MAN ENOUGH TO FORGIVE

Healing the Wounds of Fatherhood Abandonment

MAN ENOUGH TO FORGIVE

Copyrights © and Trademarks ® 2023 by John Smithbaker

ISBN 978-1-952144-16-5

All rights reserved worldwide.

First Edition

Bible passages are taken from either the New American Standard, New International Version and each of their respective copyrights.

No portion of this publication may be reproduced, stored in a retrieval system, distributed, or transmitted in any form or by any means, including photocopying, recording, or other electronic or mechanical methods, without the prior written permission of the publisher, except as provided for by the USA copyright law.

For information about permission to reproduce selection from this book must be in writing. Written permissions must be from John J. Smithbaker.

For information about special discounts for bulk purchases, please contact John Smithbaker at 844-472-4241, or info@fathersinthefield.com.

Published by Dunham Books
6111 W. Plano Pkwy., Suite 2200
Plano, TX 75093
www.dunhamandcompany.com

Printed in the United States of America

Be the man God intended you to be…

Journey Steps

CONTENTS

Prelude:	Why Write Man Enough to Forgive?	8
Foreword:	Onward Christian Solder: Lt. Col. Allen West	12
Welcome:	Introduction	17

Series One: *The Father Wound* — 24

Chapter 1:	The King David in You	26
Chapter 2:	Biblical Forgiveness	45
Chapter 3:	Defining Fatherhood Abandonment	62

Series Two: *The Battle for the Truth* — 85

Chapter 4:	The Lies of Fatherlessness	87
Chapter 5:	The Truth about How My Heavenly Father Sees Me	101
Chapter 6:	The Fatherless Man I Became	113

Series Three: *The Walking Wounded* — 126

Chapter 7:	Understanding Unforgiveness	128
Chapter 8:	My Fatherlessness Affects/Affected Everyone around Me	141
Chapter 9:	Dealing with the Emotional Hurts	163

Series Four: *The Man God Intended You to Be* — 183

Chapter 10:	Following Jesus – Forgiving Your Father	185
Chapter 11:	Being the Man of God You Were Created to Be	204
Chapter 12:	Your Forgiveness Letter	222
Appendix:	Forgiveness Letter example	234
	Personal Study Journal	238

Dedication

Next only to my adoption into the Lord's heavenly family, Jesus' most excellent gift to me is the precious Bride of my youth, Tracey Smithbaker.

She has loved me truly since we made our marital vows to one another over thirty years ago. And oh, how I love her.

Tracey has excelled as a full-time mom to our children and as my Bride. She thrives being there to nurture, comfort, encourage, and spoil all of us with her delicious meals. Tracey expresses her care and commitment to us in many ways each day. My precious Bride has always partnered with me in marriage, business, and ministry.

She helped fulfill my childhood dream of creating a peaceful, safe, and loving home - a sanctuary from the hostile and chaotic world. Our home has been a secure and protected place of rest.

Any celebration of the accomplishments and impact achieved from my personal, professional, or ministry work would be shallow and hollow without Tracey to share in it. I cannot imagine life without her – the helpmate so often described in the God's Word.

In honor of the Bride of my youth, Tracey, I dedicate this book to the men whom I pray will read it and be motivated to forgive. Thank you for forgiving me so many times. Thank you, Jesus, for her.

Acknowledgment

As we mature in Christ, we begin to really see the impact of God's providence and His plan in the story of our lives. It's incredible how He knits souls together to help shape and mold us into the person we are today.

There are a multitude of brothers and sisters whom I wish I could go back and say, "thank you for caring for me." I've been blessed by so many who have helped and guided me, corrected me, and courageously invested the time to share "Truth." I have come to believe that sharing the *Truth in Love* is a biblically commanded act and how we best care for one another. My fatherless journey was wrought with mistakes, hurts, and brokenness. However, throughout the journey of my spiritual maturation my Heavenly Father *always* had a plan to grow me into the man He intended. It is a perfect plan and living it out has brought Him the glory that only He deserves.

My writing projects are challenging and are not the apex of my natural gifting. Instead, I labor through writing with extra discipline, and it takes a toll on me because the stakes of this work are high, and I seek excellence in all work for the Lord. While I have complete clarity of the content scope to express, a good editor can help bring the presentation forward. I want to thank Michael Tomlinson for his faithful help in my writing endeavors, polishing my words without eliminating my straightforward, unvarnished approach. MT has helped me serve the Kingdom and the fatherless better and I'm eternally grateful.

Prelude

Why Write *Man Enough to Forgive*?

Perhaps more than ever in the history of our nation, Jesus Christ's Word and wisdom are counter-cultural. Man's "reason" is ruling the day.

At every turn the world is actively pushing aside, ignoring, and with an incomprehensible arrogance trying to manipulate Almighty God's unchanging Truths.

Today, absolute Truth has no place in our broken and fallen land. Instead, Americans are largely deluded by self-reliance and distracted by the service of other masters. Both are false idols.

I was compelled to write this book from the insights gained in pursuit of healing my own heart-wrenching soul wound and the lessons learned coming alongside boys and men across the country who share this crippling burden.

Man Enough to Forgive needed to be written to specifically address the #1 societal issue of our time - the **FATHERLESSNESS** caused by divorce or the abandonment, absenteeism, neglect, or indifference of a boy's God-ordained Pastor, Provider, and Protector – his father.

This endeavor is specifically for MEN, presented in a style geared for courageous and counter-cultural MEN. Straight forward and unvarnished for the masculine spirit, this book is inspired by the bold and unerring Truth of the Creator of Men - the genesis of Truth.

Men were born for a glorious and mission-oriented purpose.

Masculinity is God's gift to the world, to women and to children. God Himself defined men's specific purpose in the family. These roles are steeped in His Truth and do not change even amongst all the brokenness around us.

As I have traveled this remarkable country of ours to lead the national ministry of *Fathers in the Field*, we charge straight into the heart of the fatherlessness battle. We march behind enemy lines into the trenches of the broken. I have witnessed firsthand how generational fatherlessness destroys families and is fundamentally weakening our nation.

Our mission is to earnestly search for and rescue the desperately hurt, the angry, the lonely, and those pleading voices of the precious fatherless who are crying for help.

I am unabashed about calling out the spiritual battle that is being waged. We at *Fathers in the Field* are laser-focused on the deep and transformational healing that is possible through Christ Jesus, the work of the Holy Spirit, and the mobilization of the local biblical church.

Men — Look around you!

We cannot escape today's reality. Witness the carnage that constant and brutal cultural attacks on Godly masculinity and the principles of biblical fatherhood have on the next generation of men - our precious boys – while eroding the masculine identity that is critical to a healthy and thriving society.

The Heavenly Father called men to action – not to indifference or surrender.

I was forged for this war through my own growth and restoration from the fatherless wounds inflicted while growing up. Today we are strengthened by these battle scars while our ministry takes direct aim at the enemy. Make no mistake, the Devil knows what he's doing and seeks the destruction of fatherhood in route to the decimation of the family.

Victories won through faithful service and obedience to the Heavenly Father provide the inspiration to share God's bold Truth that the world tries to pervert.

Through our ministry to men and boys, including this book, we have the joy of reaching and helping heal one fatherless boy (and man) at a time. MEN get to be the strong and tender hands and feet of Jesus in communities through the local Bible-honoring church. MEN get to mobilize their unique and masculine gifts in service to God's Kingdom.

Pastors universally acknowledge that their churches are being overwhelmed with the symptoms of fatherlessness both among boys and men. Into adulthood and left undealt with, the wounds and consequences of father absence is sidelining many men from their true purpose in their families and from having impact in ministry.

Even as we serve to turn the tide of broken hearts in fatherless boys, for more than a decade I've fielded an unending stream of requests from Pastors to also help come alongside and heal *adult* fatherless boys who persist in carrying deep father wounds.

This urgent charter stems from Pastors witnessing the undeniable transformation in young boys following the steps is the key to healing – what we call the **forgiveness journey**.

Praise God for this call to extend our proven process to MEN so they too can experience restoration.

In this book and the available companion workbook journal, the ministry's proven and successful multi-year forgiveness curriculum, developed from my forgiveness journey, has now been adapted and contextualized for MEN.

Direct and to the point, *Man Enough to Forgive* is presented in the language of REAL MEN, those who don't seek excuses and those who can face the hard-truths and decisions that are presented squarely front and center. You are now at a crossroad. It's time to GET BUSY!

Prelude

Will you join me in this battle for truth in pursuit of masculine righteousness through forgiveness?

Do you understand that "qualified' answers are half-hearted, rebellious, and lack commitment? **Let your Yes be Yes** so as to bring honor to God Almighty.

The Babylonians are at the gate. We face a cruel adversary.

Righteous MEN are needed. Forgiveness is our battle cry!

Put on the full armor of God!

Charge!

John Smithbaker
Founding Servant,
Fathers in the Field Ministry

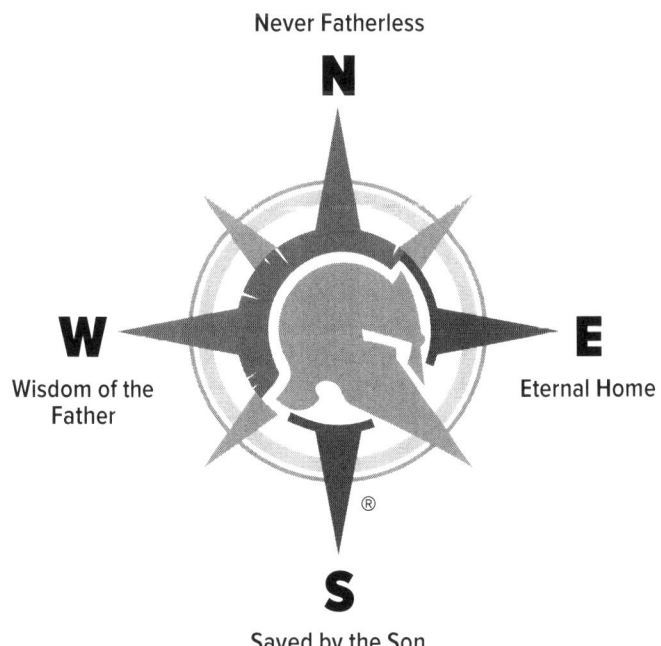

Foreword

LIEUTENANT COLONEL ALLEN B. WEST

*"When the foundations are being destroyed,
what can the righteous do?"*
Psalm 11:3 (NIV)

I cannot think of a better verse from the Bible to describe the current cultural situation in the longest running Constitutional Republic in the world, America. There are some versions of this verse that are even more descriptive of these times in which we live.

The New Living Translation version states, *"The foundations of law and order have collapsed. What can the righteous do?"*

The Amplified Bible asserts, *"If the foundations {of a Godly society} are destroyed, What can the righteous do?"*

This verse begs us to ask the question, "What is the foundation of America, a Judeo-Christian based Constitutional Republic?" The immediate response is that the foundations of our nation are the principles of classical liberalism, individual rights, freedom, and liberty. America was established on the premise that the unalienable rights of the individual, life, liberty, and the pursuit of happiness, (English political philosopher John Locke referred to this as property,) were endowed to them by the Creator, the Judeo-Christian God. This is what John Locke called Natural Rights theory. In our Declaration of Independence, Thomas Jefferson codified it and expressed it as the Laws of Nature and nature's God. However, what we are articulating here is the political philosophical foundation of America.

What is the foundation of a <u>godly society</u>, one based upon law and order?

The simple answer is this: The foundation of a godly society is the traditional nuclear family – a creation that God made in His own image – of man and woman.

It is this foundation in our society that is under critical assault. If this foundation is being progressively destroyed, what can the righteous do?

It is time to make our stand. Remember the words of God to Joshua to

> *"Be strong and of good courage, for the Lord thy*
> *God shall not leave you, nor forsake you."*

I grew up in the inner city of Atlanta, Georgia in the Old Fourth Ward neighborhood. That was the exact same neighborhood that produced Dr. Martin Luther King Jr. I was born on February 7, 1961, in a blacks-only hospital, Hughes Spalding. What is telling is that even at this time of segregation in America, and under dire social circumstances in our nation, the strength of the traditional black nuclear family prevailed.

At the time of my birth, 70% of black children had the powerful foundation of both a mom and dad in the home. On Sunday morning we all would awaken, do our morning chores, have family breakfast and off we went as families to our respective churches. It started with Sunday school for us kids. Our dads were church elders and deacons. Our moms were mothers of the church, sang in the choir, or were ushers. As kids we were encouraged (OK – we were made) to be in the children's and youth choirs. I was even an acolyte. We ate dinner as family. We were taught respect, honor, and dignity. Education was valued and stressed.

People often ask what inspired me to join the U.S. Army and be a career Army combat arms officer and veteran of several combat zones. It was my dad. My father, Herman "Buck" West Sr., was a World War II veteran and an Army Corporal. He answered the call of service at a time when this country did not see him as an equal. He encouraged and inspired my older brother to become a U.S. Marine, (yea, the black sheep of the family,) who served in combat as an infantryman in Vietnam. At the age of 15, my dad challenged me to be the first officer in our family. Today, the second officer in our family, my nephew Army Lieutenant Colonel Herman Bernard West III, is poised to command an artillery battalion. Like his uncle, Herman has several combat tours of duty and will probably end up being *the* highest-ranking member of our family.

Today, we are witnessing the foundation of family - men of honor, integrity, character, and courage - being undermined and destroyed. Today, the two-parent household in the black community is below 25%. Today, our Judeo-Christian faith heritage is under assault. Today, we are murdering our unborn babies in the womb at a genocidal rate and violence is being enacted to preserve the rituals of Moloch. Today, our little boys are being told they can be little girls. Today, our little children are being sexualized, trafficked, and exploited by adults... and yes, physically abused, abandoned, scarred for life. God save us.

Hear me now, my fellow faithful American! The foundation of our God-breathed nation is being destroyed.

What MUST the righteous do?

We must fight back, take a bold stand, and march onward to victory! It is time for the Body of Christ to accept the challenge of these times and count it all joy that these tribulations and trials have come in our time.

That is why this book, *Man Enough to Forgive*, is critical for this time.

As Christians we must break the cycle of being made victims and rise to be victors. That can only be achieved by casting off the hurt and rising above it, through forgiveness. The cancer of this current culture and society cannot not be overcome except by the grace of God and His Son, our Lord and Savior Jesus Christ. It is time we embrace the words of Romans 12:2 (NIV), "*Do not conform to the pattern of this world but be transformed by the renewing of your mind. Then you will be able to test and approve what God's will is — His good, pleasing, and perfect will*".

This means that God wants you to abandon the recipe for disaster of the world, and instead to abide in Him to find His formula of success. Healing can only begin with forgiving. Then restoration of the foundation will come. If we hold onto the darkness and hate which the world advocates, then we fall into the culture's will… not His.

My favorite book in the New Testament is Philippians. Apostle Paul's words are most encouraging and inspiring - even as he writes from prison while awaiting his execution.

I will close with Paul's sentiments from chapter three, Philippians 3:12-14 (NIV), *"Not that I have already obtained all this, or have already arrived at my goal, but I press on to take hold of that for which Christ Jesus took hold of me. Brothers and sisters, I do not consider myself yet to have taken hold of it. But one thing I do: Forgetting what is behind and straining toward what is ahead, I press on toward the goal to win the prize for which God has called me heavenward in Christ Jesus."*

When the foundations are being destroyed, what can the righteous do?

They press on toward the goal, pursuing the restoration of the foundation of our Judeo-Christian faith heritage, and fully committed to families in God's design. We march forward. We go onward, Christian Soldiers, not conforming to this culture, to this world, but transforming it by our faith and the Holy Spirit.

Lieutenant Colonel Allen B. West (US Army, Retired)
Member, 112th US Congress
Former Chairman, Republican Party of Texas

"Therefore, strengthen the hands that are weak and the knees that are feeble, and make straight paths for your feet, so that the limb which is lame may not be put out of joint, but rather be healed.

Pursue peace with all men, and the sanctification without which no one will see the Lord. See to it that no one comes short of the grace of God; that no root of bitterness springing up causes trouble, and by it many be defiled; that there be no immoral or godless person like Esau, who sold his own birthright for a single meal.

For you know that even afterwards, when he desired to inherit the blessing, he was rejected, for he found no place for repentance, though he sought for it with tears."
Hebrews 12: 12-17 (NASB)

Welcome Introduction

Book introductions can laborious because the author is attempting to tell you why you should continue to read the book. They are often filled with facts and compelling stories with hopes you'll read on.

This is not one of those introductions. I am going to be upfront, clear, and direct so that you will know exactly how to engage and benefit most as you courageously put the principles and practical steps outlined here to work in your masculine Faith journey.

Here is the first direct statement addressing the Scripture from Hebrews on the prior page. A profound truth with an overarching meaning to our Christian sanctification as we review the command to forgive others. To paraphrase a few Commentaries on these verses, believers are exhorted to <u>act upon</u> divine truths – not just to intellectually know about them.

Truth which is known but not faithfully obeyed becomes a judgment rather than a benefit.

Goals of *Man Enough to Forgive*:

- To explain biblical forgiveness and help you see the link between God's forgiveness of us and how we are to forgive others.
- To help you identify and acknowledge the lies you came to believe because of your father's absence.
- To help you better understand how your earthly father failed and why it matters in your life.

- To help you to understand and admit your reluctance to truly forgive your father for abandoning you and how that has shaped your life.
- For you to truly believe that you were born for a glorious purpose, that you are not a mistake or garbage that is thrown away.
- For you to acknowledge that the sin of unforgiveness is just as terrible and wrong as the sin of abandonment. This is a bitter pill to swallow, I know, but it will be key to the freedom and grace you'll experience in the process of both forgiveness and being forgiven.
- To help you be open to the Truth of forgiveness.
- For you to open the doors of your head and heart to understand and admit that forgiveness requires the work of the Holy Spirit in your life.
- For you to understand that the end goal is about healing your abandonment wound, which means forgiving your earthly father. For once, <u>you</u> and <u>your needs</u> are the focus and central figure of this story!
- To help you come to a place where you can know if you have truly forgiven your earthly father and have stopped allowing the Devil to use your Dad's sin of abandonment to control your attitude towards your father.
- To help you on the path to becoming the MAN that God intended you to be, in and through Christ, even in this broken and fallen world.
- Enable you to get back onto the spiritual battlefield boldly declaring your righteous role in our King's brotherhood, in your family, in your home church, at work, and for the next generation of Pastors, Providers, and Protectors.

While this book will be helpful to all fatherless men, it only finds its true success for *Christian* men.

To truly forgive your earthly father you must first understand your own sin and the forgiveness from your Heavenly Father - found only in Jesus Christ. When you repent of your sin and place your faith in Christ for salvation, you receive the Holy Spirit; it is through His power and work in your life that you will gain the ability to truly forgive.

This concept is discussed in greater detail throughout *Man Enough to Forgive*. Understanding that the assistance of the Holy Spirit's ministry is needed to forgive is vital to your moving forward in the study.

This book is designed to help you identify the full scope of what it means to be fatherless, and more importantly, to begin the process of healing. Every man has a different learning style. There will be some information that may be more interesting to you and aligned with your experience than others.

However, it is all important.

I'll walk you through a prescribed process that has helped me, many men, and fatherless boys to achieve the goals stated above. With this in mind, this book is laid out in chapters that are progressive in the overall healing and forgiving process we'll tackle together.

Also, please prayerfully consider going through the companion **Personal Study Journal / Men's Study** that helps walk you through this forgiveness process and challenges you on levels you have not thought about in this journey.

God's trustworthy Word is our Guide in this forgiveness journey.

YOUR PATH TO SUCCESS

A **QUICK START** section leads each chapter as an overview of the key points contained therein.

Think of it as a view from 30,000 feet up of the coming discussion, or the minimum information needed to get your key in the ignition and the engine started. It's for those men who just want to be told what is wrong and how to fix it.

It is designed to be quick in the answer department – but be prepared – with brevity will come hard or raw truths that may be difficult to hear.

That is followed by the **ROAD MAP**, a more detailed guide to the critically important issues that impact this complex topic.

It will help you better understand why you think, feel, and react the way you do. It is designed to help you delve deeply into the "*why*" so that you can confidently transition into the "how" and be ready to make changes in your life. You'll be blown away by the connections between these events in your life and how influential they are to your behavior.

The **NEXT STEPS** section at the end of each chapter is where you'll begin to take action. You'll be asked to reflect, to consider key concepts from the chapter, and to make powerful associations with your own life's experiences that will help you begin the healing process.

Take the time to write down your answers so that when your heart is ready to begin the journey of forgiving your earthly father you can hit the ground running.

As a man who's in control of his own behavior, you are entitled to forego answering these questions for yourself or to jump around in any order that you want. But for the best results I highly encourage you to do them in the order and fashion presented.

GET ROLLING: The Companion Journal to this book (see the reference at the end of the book).

PERSONAL STUDY JOURNAL - A profound, yet simple approach to thinking through and guiding your emotional thoughts and memories within the framework of God's Truths. This study journal is crafted to become a keep sake for you and even a generational legacy of your faithful journey following your Lord and Savior's example. It is thoughtfully organized to help you process the various and challenging steps in your Forgiveness Letter endeavor to keep you on track in fulfilling your commitment.

I would highly encourage you to use this companion **Personal Study Journal**, its online video and podcast messages to incorporate a structured process in this forgiveness journey and hear added insights and stories. Our hope is that you are involved in a men's study group where you will have godly support and further discussions to deepen your forgiveness understanding and follow-through.

With the help of the Holy Spirit, in Chapter 12, I will help you compile your answers from the previous chapters and begin the process of writing your letter. You may have a strong resistance to doing this or even to taking the time to work through these sections in the book because you believe what your dad did is unforgivable.

This is a classic emotional response and natural. But we'll transcend that limitation together.

As men, sometimes we dig our heels in and refuse to be moved from our position when we determine something is justified or that wrong has been done to us. Yet as a Christian you are commanded by God to forgive others.

You should not claim Christ and remain in a position of unforgiveness towards another human being.

> *"And when you stand praying, if you hold anything against anyone, forgive them so your Father in heaven may forgive you your sins."*
> Mark 11:25 (NASB)

Finally, at the end of each chapter I have included the **SCRIPTURE REFERENCES** presented in each.

There is such incredible wisdom and richness in God's Word. Not only is it a practical guide to soul health and fulfillment in this life while preparing us for an eternity in Heaven with our Savior, but it provides relevant context to every situation and feeling in the human experience. At any given time we need not wonder how to successfully navigate the Christian life, we can simply find examples and the guidance of our Heavenly Father in the Bible.

Don't miss this next point.

It's my commitment to you: When you *truly forgive* your earthly father for abandoning you and his fatherhood roles, the deep wound that's impacted your life so greatly until today can be healed.

You can expect that the scars caused by prior wounds will still exist and sometimes they'll get bumped and cause some tears, but that *festering* wound will be healed. You will likely sometimes feel disappointed, be confronted with unfulfilled dreams or missed opportunities or even feel a sadness of this hurt.

But you can be confident of this: the bitterness and anger that were caused by it will be gone.

Unlike the unearned gift of salvation that is offered *without* your work and *without* any possible exchange of value with the Father, your understanding of the nature of forgiveness will be directly related to your openness, to your spiritual receptivity, to your spiritual maturity, and to you having the courage to return to the platform of pain (temporarily) in order to transcend it with authenticity (permanently).

Crucially, biblical understanding is paramount for your forgiveness to stick. Growing in maturity to understand biblical forgiveness is your decision. You're making that proactive, productive, and powerful choice here and now.

It is God's command to forgive in imitation of His forgiveness of your sins. If we expect Jesus to forgive us, then we need to forgive.

The most difficult part of the process outlined within *Man Enough to Forgive* is not simply writing a letter of forgiveness to your earthly father, but rather gaining a deep understanding of biblical forgiveness and obeying God's command to forgive.

If you claim salvation in Christ and yet find yourself digging in your heels of rebellion, the very first step will be to specifically ask the Holy Spirit to change your heart and give you the strength to obey.

Remember, true forgiveness is an act of the Holy Spirit and must be done by a follower of Christ. Otherwise you are just going through the motions in order to feel better about yourself, so why waste the time?

While I am neither your earthly or heavenly father, I *am* your brother in Christ and I have been called to be your support system, your coach, and your guide in this process. This is the way of biblically-driven personal development – of growth and of fellowship.

It's the way Jesus himself taught. What better an example to follow?

<u>I am so proud of you</u>. You're already among an **elite group of Christian men** willing to do the hard things in their life to experience the tremendous blessings and grace that your Heavenly Father intended for your life.

I stand by you and we'll fight this battle together.

Let's get going!

> *"God's work, done God's way will never lack God's supplies."*
>
> Hudson Taylor

The Father Wound

SERIES ONE

Stop the Excuses!

Taking Bold Action to Become the Man God Intended You to Be.

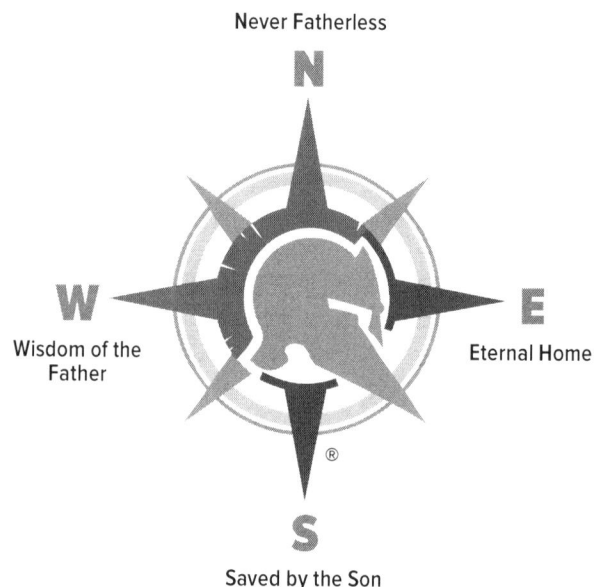

fortitude

[for·ti·tude] **noun**

Strength of mind that enables a person to encounter danger or bear pain or adversity with courage.

CHAPTER ONE

The King David in You

"For you have not received a spirit of slavery leading to fear again, but you have received a spirit of adoption as sons by which we cry out, **"Abba! Father!"** Romans 8:15 (NASB)

| Quick Start |

Generational fatherlessness and the impact of boys carrying debilitating wounds into adulthood is a bigger problem today than ever. However, it's not a contemporary condition or one manifest solely in Western society. It's an issue as old as humanity itself.

You need not look far in the Bible to find evidence of this sin and how it not only impacts families, but whole lineages of people from the earliest tribes of Israel to today. You might be surprised by some of the non-obvious examples and how the fatherhood wound is present in even some of history's most revered Christian warrior men.

Take David for example. Yes, *that* David; King David whom the Heavenly Father calls "a man after God's own heart" - *twice*.

David wrote most of the Psalms and one in particular stands out as he cries out to his Heavenly Father to not turn from him, not to hide His face from him. Psalms 27:10 ESV.

"For my father and my mother have forsaken me, but the Lord will take me in."

Knowing as we do that David *also* had major life blunders, significant sin for which he had to repent and be forgiven before *he* could be the man God called him to be, it is clear that being a person after God's own heart does not mean perfection. Nobody is perfect, except Jesus.

David's father wound began early in his story. Imagine living in David's day and the importance of men's role as leaders in the family, in the tribe, and even ruling over kingdoms.

As Jesse considered whom among his sons had the "right stuff" and would be considered by Samuel to potentially to serve as king, he called his sons to the front line but abandoned David, leaving him behind.

David, young and diminutive, wasn't even considered. Did not make the list. Imagine that, in perhaps a young man's most important moment he was completely overlooked by his father. Jesse didn't see in David what God did.

That event alone could be enough to define a young man, instilling in him a fierce bitterness that could cripple his self-worth forevermore. God had other plans though. God gave David a heart of forgiveness (David did whatever God wanted him to do. Part of God's Will is to have us forgive. Acts 13:22), so David could recognize and address the wounds, even unforgiveness; thereby, he could overcome them. The Holy Spirit came over David and he was blessed.

In David's story it is important to recognize that spiritual maturation and becoming the man God meant you to be isn't a one-and-done process. While David forgave his earthly father and opened himself to the Lord's vision for his life, he still messed up – big time.

Like each of us men, David's first and most crucial ministry obligation was to be the Pastor, Provider, and Protector of his family. Just because the Lord bestowed kingship over Israel, victory over his enemies, and used David in and through his sins, does not mean there were not severe consequences to David's unrighteous, out-of-God's-will actions. David carried his father wound and sin into his kingship, marriage, fatherhood, family, friendships, and leadership.

Have you thought critically about the devastating consequences of a father's sin and how it affects a family, a son, a community, a nation, and the next generation? By any standards, let alone the standards of God Almighty, King David was a *terrible* father, and it had a profound impact on his family, his children, and on Israel.

David was a selfish father. David was an absent father. David was an adulterer. David was a weak father. David provoked anger in his children. In many ways, David was a poor role model.

How more obvious can it be? When families tear apart and so-called modern wisdom drifts from biblical standards, it has grave effects extending far beyond our own families.

For your good and the good of this and future generations of your family, repent of your sins. Through earnest prayer ask God to open your mind and heart and receive His kingdom wisdom concerning the devastating and inevitable consequences of sin when His most holy plan for marriage and fatherhood are not followed.

David is no different than YOU. David is no different than YOUR father.

King David and those closest to David did not escape those consequences. David's son and all his children did not escape the consequences of their father's sin. God is not a liar.

There are always consequences to sin. Always.

The David in You

Just as God allows evil in the world, he allows us to be healed and restored. He helps us to be redeemed before the witness of others. Men look at outside appearances. God looks at the heart and what we do to live in His blessing and to make true His vision.

In this broken and fallen world you too can be a David. Hear the words, well done good and faithful servant. We're all capable of it. Forgiveness was fundamental to David's legacy, as it is to yours. David forgave much and was forgiven much. Same for you.

That's what *Man Enough to Forgive* is all about. It's not just about knowing how to forgive. Knowledge is earthly. But wisdom... wisdom comes from God. My greatest prayer is that you hear the Lord's heart here because you are man enough. I'm asking you to look beyond worldly knowledge so you can receive and act upon that spiritual wisdom.

| Road Map |

There are always consequences to sin. ALWAYS.

We often hear that "God can do anything." In actuality, this casually accepted premise is not accurate at all and undergirds the premise of how we and our culture view men, masculinity, the precious role of fathers, husbands, and the father wound.

One thing that God, the Heavenly Father, cannot do - is lie.

"I am *fine*." In their bravado, I hear this from men all the time. By stating this we are indirectly shouting out to the world that Jesus is not a Man of His word. We are calling God a Liar. Worse, we are minimizing the need for Jesus' painful death on the cross.

The purpose of *Man Enough to Forgive* is to boldly deal with our wounds and to forgive our earthly father.

As we consider how to do this, have you ever thought about the father wound that King David had to endure? David even cried out in anguish to the Lord that his father had forsaken him (Psalm 27:10). How it shaped him as a man? How it affected his mindset and behavior from fatherhood to marriage? How it impacted his family's generational legacy?

Let's explore David's earthly father wound for a moment since it is so rarely, if ever, highlighted in the telling of the life story of David.

Simply stated, David was overlooked, ignored, undervalued, did not measure-up, and was deemed unworthy by his father. You see, I understand the wound of being abandoned by a father. And I too had to bear all of those painful slights and put-downs as a reflection of what my father must have believed about me. Ouch!

Fortunately, I did *not* have to endure daily torment by my father's hand like David did - the countless cuts to my soul in witness of my family, brothers, and friends. How that public humiliation must have stung young David.

David was the youngest of his father, Jesse's, eight sons. So, while he was naturally trying to measure up to his older brothers, David was further demeaned by his father's shameless put-downs. No doubt, David caught the subtle and not-so-subtle jabs. It is not only the words a father uses that can wound, but also the words that are *not offered* to affirm and speak life into a young, growing boy with an impressionable soul.

Maybe it was because of David's smaller size that his dad did not think he was strong, tough, or *Man Enough*. Perhaps Jesse gave up on David because he acted differently from his brothers. Or it could be that David became weary of always falling short of the ideal shape of his father's desired mold. Possibly David's father did not value the gifts God gave him. Very likely, Jesse was more concerned with his selfish ambitions and conforming to the world's standards, instead of respecting and honoring our Heavenly Father's virtues.

All we know for sure is that David suffered the shame and sins of his father, both privately and in public. God's Word makes this abundantly clear. When the Lord's prophet, Samuel, received instructions to go to Jesse the Bethlehemite, "for I have selected a king for myself among his sons," Samuel and the town elders held a large consecration ceremony where many must have attended. Jesse invited every one of his sons to the ceremony, except David.

Not only did David's father not invite him for kingship consideration but he must not have respected his son enough to bring him along to this extraordinary, exceedingly special God instructed event.

> *"So Samuel did what the Lord said and came to Bethlehem. And the elders of the city came trembling to meet him and said, "Do you come in peace?" He said, "In peace; I have come to sacrifice to the Lord. Consecrate yourselves and come with me to the sacrifice." He also consecrated Jesse and his sons and invited them to the sacrifice."'*
> 1 Samuel 16:4-5 (NASB)

Just imagine the scene. Consider the gossip and whispering about why David was not even invited to this event. Think about how Jesse's humiliation of David impacted his other sons' perception and what the community must have thought about David. Compounding his pain, the stigma on David's precious soul would have been devastating. Being abandoned at such a special time in this family's life would bring most to their end.

Furthering the insult and deepening David's father wound, Samuel looked out to evaluate each of the brothers in the order Jesse thought his sons should be considered as king. David was not among them. Upon completing his review, Samuel providentially knew that the one *God* choose was not there. He then asked David's father if there were any others? Jesse must have mentioned David in a perplexed manner. David's father discouraged Samuel, "you do not want David; he's filthy and working."

David was simply not like his brothers, no matter how much his father tried to mold him, and David was reminded of this daily.

> *"When they entered, he looked at Eliab and thought, 'Surely the Lord's anointed is before Him.' But the Lord said to Samuel, 'Do not look at his appearance or at the height of his stature, because I have rejected him; for God sees not as man sees, for man looks at the outward appearance, but the Lord looks at the heart.' Then Jesse called Abinadab and made him pass before Samuel.*
>
> *And he said, 'The Lord has not chosen this one either.' Next, Jesse made Shammah pass by. And he said, 'The Lord has not chosen this*

one either.' Thus, Jesse made seven of his sons pass before Samuel. But Samuel said to Jesse, 'The Lord has not chosen these.' And Samuel said to Jesse, 'Are these all the children?' And he said, 'There remains yet the youngest, and behold, he is tending the sheep.' Then Samuel said to Jesse, Send and bring him; for we will not sit down until he comes here.'

David Anointed

So he sent and brought him in. Now he was ruddy, with beautiful eyes and a handsome appearance. And the Lord said, 'Arise, anoint him; for this is he.' Then Samuel took the horn of oil and anointed him in the midst of his brothers; and the Spirit of the Lord came mightily upon David from that day forward. And Samuel arose and went to Ramah." 1 Samuel 6 – 13 (NASB)

Some may not see it, but it is as clear as day to me. We have to look through the lens of a child; an impressionable young soul.

More damaging than the deeply wounding insults David had to endure, he was *left behind* by his father. **David's father forsake/*abandoned* him** (Psalm 27:10). No wonder young David turned to God to fill his fatherless void. David had deep yearnings that we <u>all</u> have as young boys - to be valued by a father and shepherded into manhood.

Let's think about this. Why did God Almighty call David, "a man after my own heart"?

I founded a ministry, *Fathers in the Field*, nearly two decades ago to pair wounded fatherless boys with godly Christian mentor fathers. Through the local church, Christ's bride. I know from both personal experience and though the work of our ministry that wounded fatherless boys suffer in private. Though tough and sometimes calloused on the outside, they cry out in pain into their pillows at night. They plea for help in many ways. They wander around deeply hurt, but nobody notices. They rebel in anger to let the world know about the pain they are suffering.

Or, they become overachievers trying to prove their worthiness. David was an overachiever and would eventually put his selfish desires ahead of his personal responsibilities to his family and his children.

I believe the Heavenly Father heard the cries of David in all of his loneliness in the wilderness. God has made clear that He hears the pleas of the widow and fatherless in their distress. As expressed in more than one hundred verses in the Bible, God's heart beats for the fatherless.

Furthermore, the Lord uses people like David, like you, whom this fallen world discards as worthless. They forsake you for not meeting its early, man-made standards. God uses the broken, the sinful, the weak, so *no one* can steal God's glory.

I imagine David could not talk with his dad, and his brothers also looked down upon him, believing what their father thought about him. How isolating that must have been. David was alone and a loner in the desert, tending sheep. In the wilderness, David honed his righteous masculinity, leadership skills, and communed with God. He brought his hurt, pain, and the despair of not being valued to the feet of his Heavenly Father, who in turn showed David the kind of fatherly love and mercy he desperately needed.

David did not hide from his pain. Instead, he was open, authentic, transparent, and vulnerable with his Abba Father.

As we know from David's many Psalms, he had a contrite and repentant heart. He acknowledged his sins against a Holy God. David did not complain or blame others, but rightfully confessed his sin. He humbled himself and asked God for help. David understood that all God's people face adversity. David was *Man Enough* to ask his Heavenly Father to reveal the sin in his life and was grateful when God disciplined him because he understood that was the Lord demonstrating His love.

David <u>must</u> have had a forgiving heart towards his earthly father because he did not make excuses for him. Instead, he understood the broken world we all have to navigate.

This is the core message of *Man Enough to Forgive*. And this is why I firmly believe God blessed David in so many ways, recognizing David as a man after His own heart.

Regardless of the situation, hardship is always a powerful tool in the Lord's hands to draw you closer to Him when you cooperate with how He wants to use it in your life. When we try to justify or minimize the wounds to our soul as "OK" or say, "it's in the past," or, "our father did as best as possible," we are not honest with the reality of the destructive nature of sin. We are saying that we are willing to settle for this broken world's standard of 'good enough' and are denying the goodness and perfection of our Creator, our King, our Savior, and our Heavenly Father.

The hurting world needs to understand the consequences of sin and the need for a forgiving Savior just like David did.

> *"But the Lord said to Samuel, 'Do not look at his appearance or at the height of his stature, because I have rejected him; for God sees not as man sees, for man looks at the outward appearance, but the Lord looks at the heart."* 1 Samuel 16:7 (NASB)

When we pretend to be unharmed or do not acknowledge God's holy plan, our witness confuses the life-giving words of the Creator that we are trying to share with a hurting and dying world.

We do ourselves and others no favor by making excuses that minimize our pain or ignores the past in order to cope with the consequences of not having a father who fulfilled the divine, spiritual or practical roles of Pastor, Provider, and Protector. Our soul yearns to be fully led into manhood by a healthy, complete shepherd <u>in</u> all of the roles. Not just one, or two. We're not being courageous or manly when we excuse our wrongful actions or inactions because "we are fine." Fine is not holy. Fine is far, far from it.

Fine is the lie of the wounded.

In prideful defiance of these truths, some will say that their curse was a blessing. In defense of their damaged self-worth they may have convinced themselves that what they experienced as a result of their father's shortcomings, absence, or abuse motivated them to prove him wrong and themselves worthy. They may even believe that without such motivation to overcome, they would not have achieved or accomplished much.

All these manmade thoughts and justifications are, in essence, calling our Holy God a liar. That His divine plan, His orderly command for sex within the covenant of marriage, His Holy structure for family, and His foundational role of righteous masculinity in boys' development to manhood are just ideals or hopeful aspirations. In fact, these are holy, perfectly ordered plans to follow.

My brother, it is pure and simple. Know that God is not a liar, ever. As I stated before, there are ALWAYS consequences to our sin and our father's sin. Our body and our mind are different than our soul. Sin ALWAYS affects the soul and produces negative consequences - even if we do not see them, feel them, or acknowledge this rebellion.

When we read the Bible and learn about King David, we typically hear about the courageous young warrior who defeated Goliath. We hear about David as mighty King for the people of Israel. These are true, of course. But we should also see a little bit of David in <u>ourselves</u> as we grow in our Christian faith and recognize the brokenness we all face in confronting this fallen land as sojourners.

> We empathize with David when we learn about his struggle with sin.
>
> We understand David when he admits his flaws.
>
> We sympathize with David when we hear of his pleas for help in his distress.
>
> We weep with David when he feels God does not hear his prayers.
>
> We identify with David's anger as friends betray him.
>
> We are thankful for David's redemption, since he was a murderer and God still forgave him.

We commend David's authentic transparency in writing his Psalms during his abandonment.

We are inspired that David's suffering did not defeat him.

We worship along with David as he gives glory to God Almighty.

We are in awe and honor David as we learn how God Himself referred to him as a "man after His (God's) own heart."

We are sad for David when the Lord told him he could not build God's temple because he had blood on his hands.

We are hopeful to learn God still used David to accomplish great things for His glory.

And, as we grow spiritually toward our Heavenly Father, we see David within us more and more.

There is no doubt that God Almighty used David in powerful ways for His glory and the Kingdom's advancement. Remember, God neither sins nor is the father of lies, but allows sin to ultimately bring Himself glory. Most assuredly, God does not let sin deter His Sovereign redemptive plan for His adopted children. What Satan meant for evil, God uses it for His good.

> *"Daniel said, 'Let the name of God be blessed forever and ever, for wisdom and power belong to Him. 'It is He who changes the times and the epochs; He removes kings and establishes kings; He gives wisdom to wise men and knowledge to men of understanding. 'It is He who reveals the profound and hidden things; He knows what is in the darkness, And the light dwells with Him.*
>
> *'To You, O God of my fathers, I give thanks, and praise, For You, have given me wisdom and power; Even now You have made known to me what we requested of You, for You have made known to us the king's matter."* Daniel 2:20-23 (NASB)

King David is among the all-time great patriarchs of the Old Testament. He accomplished incredible feats for God and Israel. He united the twelve fractured Tribes of Israel and strengthened the Jewish nation's faith with his governance as King. Young King David won many battles in God's providence. David is mentioned and referred to numerous times in God's Word. He amassed and wrote many of the Psalms and disseminated this prayer-book of Israel.

Maybe the most extraordinary and significant of David's blessings was that the Heavenly Father choose David to be in the lineage of His only Son, Jesus. David held a unique place in the larger story of the Kingdom, being connected to Jesus and Him to David. One of Christ's most well-known titles was "Son of David." Indeed, David holds an exceptional place in our Christian heritage, in God's divine plan, and was used mightily to bring God glory.

BUT, does that mean David avoided or was exempt from the consequences of his father's sins or his sins? Did those close to him - his family, his children, or even his son escape the consequences of David's sin as a husband and father? No.

Like each of us men, David's first and most crucial ministry obligation was to be the Pastor, Provider, and Protector of his family. Just because the Lord bestowed kingship over Israel, victory over his enemies, and used David in and through his sins, does not mean there were not severe consequences to David's unrighteous, out-of-God's-will actions. David carried his father wound and sin into his kingship, marriage, fatherhood, family, friendships, and leadership.

Have you thought critically about the devastating consequences of a father's sin and how it affects a family, a son, a community, a nation, and the next generation?

By any standards, let alone the standards of God Almighty, King David was a *terrible* father, and it had a profound impact on his family, his children, and on Israel.

David was a **selfish father.** Like many of today's fathers and husbands, David failed in his primary responsibilities and ministry to be the Pastor, Provider, and Protector of his family. David was more concerned about his career as king than in being an involved and present father.

David was an **absent father**. Having to juggle children from many wives compromised and divided his attention further. Children naturally become resentful, angry, and sad because of a father's inaction, lack of involvement, and for not being shepherded into adulthood and manhood. So many different family dynamics were thrust into children's lives and the royal family structure.

David was an **adulterer**. In addition to cheating with the high-profile mistress, Bethsheba, David also had more than eight wives and many sons.

Please do not buy into excuses for David's sin because he was a king or that was the cultural norm of his day. This is a shameful minimization of God's Holy Word and defies the desperate need for forgiveness through Jesus' sacrifice and death on the Cross. God Almighty made his design and rules crystal clear from the beginning with His creation of man and woman.

> *"For this reason, a man shall leave his father and his mother, and be joined to his wife; and they shall become one flesh."*
> Genesis 2:24 (NASB)

When God's order, His divine plan for marriage and family, and His direction for the shepherding of precious children is diverted, it only brings sadness, devastation, and death. David's sins not only brought destruction to his family but to Israel. There is ALWAYS a consequence when God's plan is not followed. That is why God HATES divorce.

> *"For I hate divorce, says the Lord, the God of Israel..."*
> Malachi 2:16 (NASB)

Although parents may try to defend their rationale for divorce as "we are better off" or "because we're better off, the kids or better off too," this minimizes or completely disregards God's truths and God's perfect plan.

David was a **weak father**. When families are split, divided, or confused through multiple marriages, divorces, etc. many parents become weak, intentionally or unintentionally, concerning upholding discipline and other core responsibilities, largely due to their absence and guilt.

Sadly, in many broken and so-called blended families, the children and stepsiblings are shuffled off to be cared for by strangers, which contributes to the exponentially growing rate of child sexual abuse. David's family is no exception. His firstborn son and likely heir, Amnon, grew desirous of and eventually raped his half-sister, Tamar.

According to the Scriptures, David was outraged by the rape but did not act on it given his love for his firstborn son. But as we know, love without discipline is not love at all. The love of a father must stand up for righteousness. Amnon committed a grave sin and should have been held to account.

> *"Then Absalom, her brother, said to her, 'Has Amnon your brother been with you? But now keep silent, my sister, he is your brother; do not take this matter to heart.' So Tamar remained and was desolate in her brother Absalom's house. Now when King David heard of all these matters, he was very angry."* 2 Samuel 13:20-21 (NASB)

David **provoked anger** in his children. Given David's inaction, one of David's other sons, the full brother of Tamar, Absalom, was furious and outraged at the atrocity committed to his sister.

> *"Fathers, do not provoke your children to anger, but bring them up in the discipline and instruction of the Lord."* Ephesians 6:4 (NASB)

Absalom eventually schemed and killed Amnon. Now David lost two sons and had a daughter who had been raped. Absalom continued to grow bitter towards his father and organized a significant rebellion against David, wanting him dead. In the battle that ensued Absalom's rebellion was put down and David's army killed the son of his flesh.

> *"The king was deeply moved and went up to the chamber over the gate and wept. And thus, he said as he walked, 'O my son Absalom, my*

son, my son Absalom! Would I had died instead of you, O Absalom, my son, my son!" 2 Samuel 18:33 (NASB)

David was a **poor role model**. Like father, like son. What a legacy?! Our children often learn more from watching us than from the sermons we preach to them. The sins of a father are magnified in his children. The chaos, confusion, family strife, sibling jealousness, and unfaithfulness are all byproducts of a family's brokenness. Solomon was a wise king is some regards, but he also inherited some of David's immoralities. Solomon ended up having one thousand wives, (he loved many foreign women,) and they turned his heart towards other gods. As such, he was not devoted to the one true God. He also worshiped Moloch, the detestable god of the Ammonites, and did evil in the eyes of the Lord.

How more obvious can it be? When families tear apart and so-called modern wisdom drifts from biblical standards, it has grave effects extending far beyond our own families. We clearly see the impact of this 'modern wisdom' all around us. Divorce, remarriages, single parenthood, homosexual unions, and polygamy are all on the rise. The dysfunctional consequences are polluting our churches, communities, and our nation.

Our children - *your* children - pay the price and bear the burden of this unraveling of God's plan and rampant sin. The devastating and increasing statistics do not lie. As with ancient Israel, our nation's future is in the balance. As families go, so goes the nation.

We discussed how some men pretend that their father wound does not have profound influence on them or try to protect their egos by believing "what's in the past doesn't matter."

Would you please pause for a prayerful moment to receive some important insight, a critical encouragement, and some unavoidable truth?

Please. For your good and the good of this and future generations, repent of your sins. Through earnest prayer ask God to open your mind and heart and receive His kingdom wisdom concerning the devastating and inevitable consequences of sin when His most holy plan for marriage and fatherhood are not followed.

David is no different than YOU. David is no different than YOUR father.

He was flawed. He sinned. He did not live up to his role as Pastor, Provider, and Protector of his family. David hurt and sinned against those closest to him. David betrayed those he was 69to love the most. David's sin created generational hurt, pain, a legacy of dysfunction, and family destruction.

King David and those closest to David did not escape those consequences. David's son and all his children did not escape the consequences of their father's sin. God is not a liar.

There are ALWAYS consequences to sin.

Yes, the Heavenly Father used David in mighty ways. Yes, Jesus is from the lineage of David. And, yes, God called David a man after his own heart. Scripture clearly attests to God's love for David.

So what are the key lessons here? David had a heart for God and the Lord knew that full well. Most importantly, David acknowledged he was a wretched sinner, and apart from God he had no hope. David had a repentant heart and recognition of the need for forgiveness. And, David honored the call to forgive others and be humbled at the feet and throne of God. In the end, David had a reverential fear for God, rooted in love.

As with all of God's anointed, they are to help point us to Jesus Christ, our perfect example. We as men and husbands, are to Love our bride, as Christ Jesus perfectly loves His bride and be quick to ask forgiveness when we do not.

Like David, you've sinned. Like David, you can forgive and be forgiven. Like David, you can be used in mighty ways by your loving Heavenly Father.

No matter the struggles, the heartbreak, the setbacks, the regrets and the brokenness, you don't have to be defeated by any of it. Be *Man Enough* to view life and eternity from God's perspective and you will emerge victorious through the Abba Father-and-son relationship through the re-birth, being born-again.

Repent and forgive. You can be the man God intended you to be.

I believe in you!

| **Chapter 1: Study** |

NEXT STEPS: Working through the chapter

    a. How can you relate to King David's story?

    b. Have you grieved the wound(s) your father gave you?

    c. Was God wrong in choosing David, who he knew would sin greatly *even after* he was anointed? Was GOD wrong in knowing that David would become forevermore a model of faithfulness, of godly masculinity, of repentance, and of what it looks like to be a man after God's heart?

    d. What "truths" about *you* were formed by your earthly father's opinion of you?

    e. What are some of your non-obvious David-like traits that are beneath the surface and can be unburdened by your obedience and forgiveness of your father?

    f. What can you do now to both respond to God's calling in your life and to avoid the sin that keeps you trapped in the shadows of the past?

GET ROLLING with the <u>Companion Guide</u>: Preparation to write a *Forgiveness Letter*:

    - Utilize the *Man Enough to Forgive* Personal Study Journal workbook

| Scripture References |

1. Samuel gathers candidates to be the next king. 1 Samuel 16:4-5 (NASB)

2. Samuel selects David as the following king of Israel.
   1 Samuel 6 – 13 (NASB)

3. The Lord sees not a man's appearance, but his heart.
   1 Samuel 16:7 (NASB)

4. God's design for man and woman. Genesis 2:24 (NASB)

5. The Lord hates divorce. Malachi 2:16 (NASB)

6. David does not discipline his son Amnon for the shameful rape of his half-sister. 2 Samuel 13:20-21 (NASB)

7. Discipline children and do not provoke them to anger.
   Ephesians 6:4 (NASB)

8. David mourns after his army kills his son Amnon.
   2 Samuel 18:33 (NASB)

courage

[cour·age] **noun**

A reliance on the presence and power of God and a commitment to His commandments. Indifference is cowardliness.

CHAPTER TWO

Biblical Forgiveness

"So, as those who have been chosen of God, holy and beloved, put on a heart of compassion, kindness, humility, gentleness and patience; bearing with one another, and forgiving each other, whoever has a complaint against anyone; just as the Lord forgave you, so also should you"
Colossians 3:12-13 (NASB)

| Quick Start |

To be clear, this book was written with Christians in mind. What do I mean by this? *Man Enough to Forgive* is built on the premise that you have to experience true biblical forgiveness prior to your being able to truly forgive your earthly father.

> **Truth #1:** Biblical forgiveness is unmerited, undeserved and unearned by our actions, and is completely contingent on the life, death, and resurrection of Jesus Christ.

The Bible tells us that all people have sinned, doing what goes against God's nature, and that the punishment for sin is death.

This references not just physical and spiritual death but extends to physical and spiritual punishment in Hell for the rest of eternity. The Bible directs that if we have not received God's forgiveness in this life on earth that we will suffer the punishment for sin in the next life – via a very real and painful, never-ending existence. At death we don't cease to exist, nor do all people automatically get to go to heaven.

There are actual consequences for the entirety of our actions.

Further, the Bible tells us that our good deeds cannot offset sin. By contrast, God loved His children so much that He sent His Son to become a man, to live the perfect life that we can only aspire to, to die the death we deserve, and to demonstrate His divinity by rising from the dead. By repenting and confessing our sins and asking God to forgive us, in Christ we can have new life.

When an individual is converted and has repented of their sins and placed their hope for salvation in Jesus Christ alone, they receive the Holy Spirit. With the Holy Spirit living within the believer's heart and mind they may truly grasp the depth of Christ's forgiveness of them. This understanding, in turn, show them the path of obedience to Christ's commands to forgive others in our life. One of the most fundamental and important of these commands is to forgive everyone who has wronged you.

When questioned by His disciples on how to pray, Jesus responded by telling them to:

> *"Pray, then, in this way:*
> *'Our Father who is in heaven,*
> *Hallowed be Your name.*
> *'Your kingdom come.*
> *Your will be done,*
> *On earth as it is in heaven.*
> *'Give us this day our daily bread.*
> *'And **forgive** us our debts, as we also have **forgiven** our debtors.*
> *'And do not lead us into temptation, but deliver us from evil.*
>
> *For if you forgive others for their transgressions, your heavenly Father will also forgive you. But if you do not forgive others, then your Father will not forgive your transgressions."*
>
> Matthew 6:9-15 (NASB)

Jesus notes in this guided and perfect prayer that we are to request that God forgive us our trespasses (sins) or debts to Him in the same way that we forgive those in debt to us. Imagine if God *only* forgave your lies, hatred, lust, deceit, etc. in the same way you forgive those who have hated, lied, and mistreated you! What a terrifying thought.

Jesus was perfectly clear in what followed - if you refuse to forgive, don't expect God to forgive you.

Do you see? <u>Forgiveness is essential</u>.

While you don't earn forgiveness or salvation, you <u>do</u> play an active role in your Christian maturity, otherwise known as sanctification.

That's GOOD NEWS, right?! There's something to do here. We men love to *do* stuff!

Without the power of the Holy Spirit in your life you could never fathom how much God has forgiven you, let alone forgive others in the same way. In this, Jesus Christ stands as our example of both Godly forgiveness and human forgiveness. Being *Man Enough to Forgive* means understanding both biblical forgiveness and imitating Jesus - the model of perfect manhood. When Jesus hung on the cross for the sins of the world, He demonstrated total forgiveness and set an example for all who would call themselves His disciples.

This is why your Christian faith is fundamental to the ability to truly forgive, and thereby responding to Christ's command. And this is why this book is for you.

| Road Map |

As Christians we believe that the Bible is God's Word and that it contains everything we need to know to internalize who God is and who we are in relation to Him. The Bible tells us that God created humans in His own image (Genesis 1:26-30) and were placed in the Garden of Eden to glorify God and learn obedience. This requirement of obedience was first introduced by God's rule to not eat of the tree of the knowledge of good and evil (Genesis 2:16-17). Adam and Eve, the first people, lived in the garden and walked with God in the cool of the evening. During this time God allowed Satan, an angel and the first being to rebel against his maker, to roam the face of the earth including the Garden of Eden where Adam and Eve were. Genesis 3 recounts how Satan deceived Adam and led him into disobedience by eating of the tree of knowledge of good and evil.

The disobedience of *Adam* brought sin into the world; with sin came death and the corruption of the image of God in humanity.

> *"Therefore, just as through one man sin entered into the world, and death through sin, and so death spread to all men, because all sinned,"* Romans 5:12 (NASB)

This means that Adam's failure to be obedient brought both physical and spiritual death into the world. But wait, John. Didn't *Eve* eat the fruit first? This fact is directly counter to what most Christian men understand – believing that it was Eve who spoiled the soup. From a biblical standpoint, this unraveling began with Adam who God made His covenant with. Adam failed his wife. The event's account in Genesis tells us that Adam was there when Eve ate of the fruit but he did not intervene and stop her or take her directly to God after she sinned. Rather, he too ate of the fruit and broke the covenant with God resulting in sin entering the world.

When confronted by God regarding the broken covenant Adam refused to take responsibility, choosing to blame his wife instead.

How often do we see this most fundamental error in our own relationships? Who's fault is it? Who failed first? But here we see from the very dawn of mankind that God's charter is clear. It's the man's job to lead. Period.

Every person sins. A sinner from birth, everyone. Regardless of the magnitude or one's earthly justification everyone will experience death. Whether it is a "white lie," cheating on your taxes, hating another human being, looking lustfully at a woman, or a hundred other things that go against the Holy nature of the Creator God, each sin separates us from the Heavenly

Father. Because of His Just love and desire for the very best for His children, that's why He hates *all* our sins – and we should too.

Not one of us is without sin and our otherwise good conduct can never earn the forgiveness of God for our sins. Sin fundamentally corrupts the image of God in each of us.

I believe that the softening attitude and acceptance of sin is a powerful weapon of the Devil in our culture today. So much of society has come to accept all but the greatest of sins as "not all that bad." In fact, justification for most sin is granted not in black and white truths, but in relative comparison between sinners. Or, even in half-truths which are lies.

Imagine you are taking a flight from Miami to New York City. The pilot puts in the exact latitude and longitude coordinates of the destination into the plane's navigation system to insure you will arrive at the destination. Without sin, our natural orientation would have been towards true north, to God, because we are created in His image and designed to bring Him glory in every act of life. Sin is like entering destination coordinates that are off by one degree or more. A single degree might seem insignificant, but even small errors over time and distance will cause the plane to completely miss its destination. Now imagine that each sin pushes you off a degree, turning you slightly further away from God and from pleasing Him.

As you grow and spiritually mature and live in disobedience to the commands of God you will quickly find yourself going the *totally* wrong direction, away from God and thus away from the full life he intended for you.

If we die separated from God because of our unrepented sins and unbelief, the Bible tells us that Hell is the final place for those who don't receive salvation and forgiveness in Jesus Christ alone. God Almighty loves us so much that He became a man (Jesus Christ), who lived the perfect life of obedience, died on the cross to pay for our sin and rose from the dead so that death will have no power over sin. Our faith walk provides a wonderfully practical moral guide that identifies our sins and illustrates our deep dependence on the Father.

We can't fix our broken relationship with God by making up for shortcomings though our works. We need to be saved by Him and work out our salvation through fear and trembling. (Philippians 2:12)

The birth, life, death and resurrection of Jesus Christ sets believers free from the bonds of sin and death. The Bible says that:

> *"that if you confess with your mouth Jesus as Lord, and believe in your heart that God raised Him from the dead, you will be saved; for with the heart a person believes, resulting in righteousness, and with the mouth he confesses, resulting in salvation. For the Scripture says, 'Whoever believes in Him will not be disappointed."*
> Romans 10:9-11 (NASB)

The Bible goes on to explain that when you are born-again, your hope for salvation is in Christ alone. The old sinful person you were dies and is raised to life in Jesus Christ. It is like being reset to the correct coordinates, being reset to the original position of Adam and Eve in which you are asked to obey the commands of God and are no longer being pushed off course by your sin. This doesn't mean you will stop sinning. Unfortunately, we still live in a world affected by sin and death.

However, you can repent of sin and find endless forgiveness and fellowship with an Abba Father. As a disciple of Christ, you learn more what it means to be like Jesus, to love what He loves, and hate what He hates.

As you live in continued obedience, your behaviors and attitudes will change to reflect those of the God of Creation.

There is a caveat: This obedience does not save you. That work was done by Christ *on His adopted children's behalf.* However, obedience reflects the original design and the divine purpose that is being restored in you through the Holy Spirit. There is much more to the topics of eternal salvation in Christ, and I encourage you to connect with a local, biblically sound pastor to gain greater understanding of the robust theological implications.

Biblical Forgiveness

From this point forward, I am speaking <u>directly</u> to those who profess to be Christians.

If you are not yet a believer, I still encourage you to continue reading. You will struggle with the concept of forgiveness as outlined here, but so will many who profess faith in Christ.

Remember, I love you as a brother and want what is best for you. With the help of the Holy Spirit and your faithful obedience to God you can embrace biblical forgiveness and model Christ in forgiving your earthly father.

First, let's define what we mean by forgiveness.

To forgive is to pardon a debt or offense that has been committed by another against you. If you stood before a judge and were convicted of a crime but he pardoned your crime, the law would no longer enact punishment upon you or regard you as guilty. You would no longer be associated with the wrongdoing and you would be free.

To truly forgive requires that we see unforgiveness as a sin. We recount Jesus saying,

> "And He said to him, "You shall love the Lord your God with all your heart, and with all your soul, and with all your mind.' This is the great and foremost commandment. The second is like it, 'You shall love your neighbor as yourself.' On these two commandments depend the whole Law and the Prophets." Matthew 22:37-40 (NASB)

Sin breaks God's command to love Him and our neighbor, even though we have experienced Christ's love for us. It is impossible to honestly declare that we have both embraced the forgiveness of our sins, and also continue hating our brother and refuse to extend the similar forgiveness. Even if that "neighbor" is the father who abandoned his fatherly duties by leaving you, or for not fulfilling his fatherhood roles.

True forgiveness must model the biblical forgiveness we experienced in Christ who forgave our sins – without reservation and without exception.

And, hear this brother: it is joyfully done in faithful obedience.

Let me set the stage here. Picture Jesus, who was without sin or fault, as He hung from a cross - beaten, bloodied, shamed, pierced, and in agony as the burden of gravity literally tore flesh and bone from His broken frame. In that moment – as God *and* man – He did the miraculous. He forgave. Jesus even lobbied before the Heavenly Father for those who crucified Him when He said,

> *"Father, forgive them; for they do not know what they are doing."*
> Luke 23:34 (NASB)

Each of these sinners, the Romans, the Jewish leadership, and the mob had their own paths that led them to participate in the killing of the Savior (with God the Father's permission) and yet, Jesus interceded on their behalf with the Father. Jesus had committed no crime. He had not sinned in any way (Hebrews 4:15). Yet these people mocked and decimated Him as if He were the scum of the earth.

Straight talk here. My response probably would have been to ask God to kill them or allow me to rejoice in them spending eternity in Hell. Jesus' response was to forgive them and shower His enemies with love and compassion. It's a high charter, but true forgiveness asks us to follow our Savior's example.

The biblical forgiveness theme runs throughout the Bible. A great example is shown in a story Jesus told the disciples when He was instructing them on how to resolve conflict with one another. The story is related in Matthew 18:21-35 (NASB):

> *"Then Peter came and said to Him, "Lord, how often shall my brother sin against me and I forgive him? Up to seven times?" Jesus said to him, "I do not say to you, up to seven times, but up to seventy times seven.*

"For this reason the kingdom of heaven may be compared to a king who wished to settle accounts with his slaves. When he had begun to settle them, one who owed him ten thousand talents was brought to him. But since he did not have the means to repay, his lord commanded him to be sold, along with his wife and children and all that he had, and repayment to be made. So the slave fell to the ground and prostrated himself before him, saying, 'Have patience with me and I will repay you everything.'

And the lord of that slave felt compassion and released him and forgave him the debt. But that slave went out and found one of his fellow slaves who owed him a hundred denarii; and he seized him and began to choke him, saying, 'Pay back what you owe.' So his fellow slave fell to the ground and began to plead with him, saying, 'Have patience with me and I will repay you.' But he was unwilling and went and threw him in prison until he should pay back what was owed. So when his fellow slaves saw what had happened, they were deeply grieved and came and reported to their lord all that had happened.

Then summoning him, his lord said to him, 'You wicked slave, I forgave you all that debt because you pleaded with me. Should you not also have had mercy on your fellow slave, in the same way that I had mercy on you?' And his lord, moved with anger, handed him over to the torturers until he should repay all that was owed him. My heavenly Father will also do the same to you, if each of you does not forgive his brother from your heart."

The message of the story is very clear. God has forgiven us, in Jesus Christ, the huge debt our sin has earned us. The sins others commit against us, no matter how terrible, are small in comparison to the forgiveness we have received.

When we then refuse to imitate Christ and forgive the offender, how can we expect God to forgive us?

Forgiveness does not mean Reconciliation

Many Christians confuse forgiveness and reconciliation by conflating or combing them into a single concept. This is a critical distinction we must fully understand (more on this later).

So, let me state it again for good measure. Forgiveness does not mean *Reconciliation*.

Forgiveness may turn into reconciliation through the conduit of true, born-again repentance, but I am not suggesting that when one forgives they must be around an evil, dangerous, or abusive person or father. Biblical forgiveness is not dependent on an earthly reconciliation, but heavenly fellowship does require forgiveness.

Adopted through Christ Jesus Alone

Regeneration is where the Holy Spirit replaces your heart of stone with a heart of flesh. This new heart is no longer a slave to sin allowing you to extend forgiveness for what you may see as the unforgiveable sin in others or your earthly father. Our conversion testimony should be viewed and celebrated as our special adoption story into the family of the Heavenly Father. A soothing salve for the fatherless boy's soul.

In Christ Jesus' sacrifice, our sins were forgiven once for all (1 John 2:2). This is not a one-sin-at-a-time perpetuated act, but a one-time complete and definitive action for the true believer at the time of his Conversion. This specific point in time is known as Justification. One does not possess God's forgiveness until we repent and receive it by God's grace at the specific point and time even if we do not know the exact moment. The ongoing action of forgiveness experienced by the believer comes as they repent of their lessoning sins, asking for forgiveness that returns him to a life of joyful fellowship with the Heavenly Father enabled through the power of the indwelling Holy Spirit (1 John 1:9).

This on-going process in the believer is called Sanctification which continues until we are Glorified with Jesus in death or His return.

The forgiveness of the Heavenly Father for sins is always present and complete in the true believer.

GOOD NEWS! YOU'RE NEVER ALONE

The same is true when the Holy Spirit empowers you to forgive those who have hurt you, even abandoned you. You choose to imitate Christ and extend forgiveness to them, but earthly reconciliation cannot happen until they repent and receive your forgiveness. Your part is to extend Christlike forgiveness without any expectations of something in return. Their part is to acknowledge, repent, and own their sinful actions and behavior.

Focus on doing your part. Your forgiveness can't be conditional on your father's repentance or even his return into your life. Sadly, some people to whom you extend genuine Spirit-led forgiveness will never repent. In the same way, in reality, millions of people will *never* repent of their sins against God, and therefore, will not be reconciled to Christ Jesus and spend eternity tormented in Hell. But it is vital to understand that God's sovereign plan is still perfect and good.

Sin on Sin: It's a natural feeling, but not right.

We often want revenge on those who harm us, born from our hurt and anger. But our Savior wants His children to extend mercy and experience His love. Leave the discipline, or eternal punishment to Him! After all, experiencing the love of God is one of His greatest desires for all those made in His image. Our sense of justice can lead us to partially forgive others *with* a contingency that there's repentance on our terms by he who has wronged us. God, in His infinite mercy, puts no additional conditions on our repentance to Him - other than it is genuine.

We see this most vividly portrayed by Jesus, who as He hung on the cross forgave the repentant criminal hanging next to Him (Luke 23:39-49). Jesus did not demand signs of repentance but understood the authentic expression and granted reconciliation to an undeserving sinner.

What Forgiveness is not

When seen as total freedom from debt or offense, forgiveness cannot just be verbally saying that you won't harbor resentment, anger, and hatred because of the evil actions that another person has brought to your life. It must be removed from your heart and granted to them completely. Ultimately, it means giving no power to the memory of those actions. When invariably the memories come up and your heart grows angry, true forgiveness will allow you the freedom to live it out by reinforcing your commitment and you saying to yourself, "I have forgiven that hurt, and I refuse to be held captive by letting it change my behavior and attitude."

Primary Benefit: Faithful obedience to God's command to forgive.

Secondary Benefit: True freedom from the pain and offense of their past.

Forgiveness is not a <u>feeling</u>, but a conscious choice to be spiritually obedient to the command of God to love Him by imitating Him. To truly love your neighbor, you must extend him the same forgiveness God extended to you. Loving your neighbor does not mean you have to be blind to the sinful actions and desires of others, but it does require you to love your enemy as yourself, to pray for them and extend the forgiveness to them that God showed you while you were "still His enemy" (Matthew 5:44-48).

This doesn't mean you won't experience times in your life where the old hurt comes to the surface and all the heart wrenching emotions come flooding into your mind and heart. The difference is you are making a conscious effort to not let these hurts and emotions run your life. We hurt ourselves when we hold on to offense. How many times have you been bitter and defiant, roiling in resentment and maybe even hate, when the other person is blissfully unaware or unconcerned about your pain? In other words, you allow hurt and anger to punish yourself.

Forgiveness is at the heart of our relationship with Christ.

As Christians the Holy Spirit helps us to truly understand biblical forgiveness and the precious *gift* it is to extend forgiveness to others who have harmed us as a testament to our relationship with Christ.

Forgiveness is at the heart of the Gospel. We know this is a tough subject for many because of the deep, hurtful body and soul wounds that have been inflicted. And even more so because *who* dealt the pain was often the person who was supposed to protect you - even your father who should have been your protector and hero.

My hope and prayers are that you are open and *man enough* to fully understand what biblical forgiveness is and what it requires of us.

"Because it is hard" is not an excuse to skip this vital part of your spiritual maturation and development. Don't remain in the chains of unforgiven bondage, out of fellowship with the Heavenly Father, and bring doubt upon your eternal salvation. Rather, follow and model the example of forgiveness that is <u>so important</u> it was the final lesson the Son of Man taught as a human on the cross.

With the Lord's help, we pray that you are willing to ask the Holy Spirit to help you extend this forgiveness, even to your earthly father, so you can finally heal and become the man God intended for you to be. Be *man enough* to ask God Almighty for help through prayer.

My prayer suggestion. Please pray with me....

"Dear Heavenly Father,

We are in awe of you and so grateful for your goodness, justice and mercy on us, on me. We owe everything to you. Thank you for allowing me to call you Abba Father (daddy) and adopting me into your eternal family. You are all mighty and sovereign over all things great and small. This wisdom provides me with a comfort and peace beyond our understanding. We live in a broken and fallen world that is not our home. We witness so much hurt and pain that we so look forward to you setting all things right when your Son Jesus returns.

Lord Jesus, I boldly and yet, humbly ask that you extend repentance, faith and forgiveness to those who do not know you. Lord Jesus, you have forgiven me so much and I thank you for opening my eyes, renewing my mind and transforming my heart to understand this great sacrifice and suffering on your part. I pray Lord, please give me this courage, a deep sacrificially love for those who are lost, who have hurt and wronged me.

Thank you for your example on that cross. My words cannot express my soul's joyful cry of gratitude for the forgiveness granted to me. Lord, I need help in understanding how and why my dad walked away from me and my family which inflicted a wound too deep to comprehend, and a pain that has ached for so long. Holy Spirit, please provide your faithful obedience; the courage of David, a man after your own heart; and the sacrificial submission like Jesus unto His Father allowing me to forgive what, my mind says, is the unforgiveable sin. I know this is not true Lord, forgive me. Help me. Lord Jesus, my life is in your hands. Please draw me closer to you each day. Please gird me for battle to the schemes of the evil one.

Lord, God Father, please help me be the man you want me to be. A man after your own heart. In your Son's mighty, death defeating name of Jesus, I pray.

Amen!"

| **Chapter 2: Study** |

NEXT STEPS: Working through the chapter

a. This question must be asked, "have your repented of your sins and received Christ as your Lord and Savior?"

b. Do you remember when you were forgiven by Jesus and adopted as a son by the Heavenly Father?

c. Given the depth of your sins and the depth of God's grace and mercy upon you, do you recognize you continue to sin, albeit hopefully less and less?

d. Since being Born-again, have you noticed or witnessed that it is easier and you ask with more ease for forgiveness when you sin or offend others?

e. Do you have a favorite Bible verse? What is it and why is it special to you?

f. Did you recognize and fully understand the distinct and very important differences between Forgiveness and Reconciliation?

g. How did you respond to learning Forgiveness is not a feeling?

h. Are you someone who uses "it is hard" as an excuse or as motivation not to forgive others?

GET ROLLING with the <u>Companion Guide</u>: Preparation to write a *Forgiveness Letter*:

- Utilize the *Man Enough to Forgive* Personal Study Journal workbook

| Scripture References |

1. Forgiving one another Colossians 3:12-13 (NASB)

2. The Lord's Prayer. Matthew 6:9-15 (NASB)

3. God creates man in His image. Genesis 1:26-30 (NASB)

4. God's rule to not eat of the tree of knowledge of good and evil. Genesis 2:16-17 (NASB)

5. Adam brings sin into the world. Romans 5:12 (NASB)

6. We need to take fear of the Lord seriously. 2 Cor. 7:1 (NASB)

7. Believers are set free from sin and death. Romans 10:9-11 (NASB)

8. The first and second commandments. Matthew 22:37-40 (NASB)

9. Jesus asks the Heavenly Father to forgive us. Luke 23:34 (NASB)

10. Jesus is sinless. Hebrews 4:15 (NASB)

11. Jesus teaches on conflict resolution and forgiveness. Matthew 18:21-35 (NASB)

12. Our sins are forgiven once and for all. 1 John 2:2 (NASB)

13. The indwelling Holy Spirit helps us to forgive and obey. 1 John 1:9 (NASB)

14. Jesus forgives the repentant criminal on the cross. Luke 23:39-49 (NASB)

15. Love your enemies. Matthew 5:44-48 (NASB)

truth

noun

The entirety of God's Word is truth. He cannot lie. God is truth, the Spirit is truth, and Jesus is truth. Jesus is the standard.

CHAPTER THREE

Defining Fatherhood Abandonment

"Do nothing from selfishness or empty conceit, but with humility of mind regard one another as more important than yourselves;"
Philippians 2:3 (NASB)

| Quick Start |

God designed the family around the covenant of marriage. A man who refuses to make the verbal and written commitment of marriage is conveying to his children that he is willing to leave them should the family dynamic no longer be favorable to him. This is not to say that a married man won't *also* abandon his family despite the verbal and written commitment of a marriage contract, but it sends that unspoken message.

Certainly, society's perspective has shifted concerning the role of man in the family. Parenting outside the home makes the fulfillment of a man's biblical fatherly roles of Pastor, Provider, Protector <u>not possible</u>.

This is not to say that being married, or not, by itself fundamentally prohibits a man from being a caring father. However, trying to successfully live out the vital role of father while being unmarried is *not* consistent with God's plan for the family. Anytime we divert from God's plan, we cause harm to ourselves and others. Society tries to convince us otherwise.

The God-appointed, ordained roles of a father are to be the Pastor, Provider, and Protector of the home. Any father that fails his children in one or more of these roles inflicts some degree of a fatherhood abandonment wound. If not, then God is a liar since God designed these roles. In our sinful and corrupt world, the vast majority of men have experienced some type of father wound from their father through his failing in one of these critical and ordained roles.

A large part of healing your wound and writing a *Forgiveness Letter* to your father requires you to honestly evaluate how your father failed in one or more of these roles. This is challenging for some men because it is "easier" to gloss over his father's failures and to "move on with your life" than to honestly assess and critique the man who was supposed to be one's hero and model of Christian manhood. We may also feel disloyal, harsh, unkind, and even hypocritical in this process of focusing on another's shortcomings, especially if we've picked up and are repeating bad lessons.

The purpose of recognizing and openly articulating where your father failed is to see it for what it is, to begin to forgive and release those hurts, and to know the behavior so you do not repeat the behavior.

It is helpful to identify the type of father you had with one of the most commonly seen categories to understand his influence on you. I explore these categories in depth in the expanded *ROAD MAP* section: My Father Died; I Never Knew Him; Divorce; Father is in Jail; the Sporadic Father; the Father is Present, But Not Involved; the Drunk or Drugged Out Father; the Father too Busy to Care; my Father Hated Me.

You might find that several of these descriptions ring true for your father and you will need to honestly evaluate how each impacted you both when growing up and today.

Every wound hurts a boy, but pain dealt by a father is particularly damaging for both boys and men and difficult to heal. This is because our fathers hold a unique and special place as a hero in our lives. Our fathers, in a way, are meant to be a pre-cursor example of the Heavenly Father. When the cup is broken, or damaged, the soul is affected.

We work hard to protect that status for them, even if they treated us terribly. We resist and grieve that loss of status, even if they did not earn or deserve it. Many men understate the effect of these wounds to shield themselves from the pain and protect the image of their father. A powerful, and natural defense mechanism.

Other men inflate and wallow in the wound to justify their unwillingness to forgive him or to co-sign their own sin and perpetuation of his poor example. No wound is greater or less than another because every wound serves to shape us as men and requires healing. This healing comes through the power of the Holy Spirit as He helps you learn to honestly evaluate the hurt and gives you the strength to forgive the man who hurt you. It stops being your identity.

Forgiveness is not acceptance.

Forgiving your father for the wounds he caused does not excuse his behavior and may never end in reconciliation. However, forgiveness is the actual recognition that God has called us to biblically forgive and is being obedient to His command. The evidence of your forgiveness will be your willingness to write and deliver, (if possible,) the *Forgiveness Letter*. If your father still lives, is also seen in your willingness to pray regularly for him to come to a saving relationship with Jesus Christ.

Finally, forgiveness is also reflected in how you talk about your father and the hurts he caused you.

| Road Map |

A FATHER'S ROLE

God designed the family to be built upon the foundational covenant of marriage between one man and one woman. When a man refuses to make the public, official, and accountable verbal and written commitment of marriage, but instead wants only the appearance of family or the physical benefits of that relationship with a woman, he sends several powerful messages.

The first is that he does not value the woman enough to openly declare a commitment to her, leaving her wondering how committed he is to the relationship. Secondly, he is conveying to his children that he is committed to sex with their mother but is open to leaving her and them if he's no longer satisfied by the faux family arrangement.

This is not to suggest that a man won't abandon his family *just* because he has made the official commitment of marriage, but when they are old enough to understand, his children will clearly see his lack of true commitment. Finally, it makes the exercising of his biblical fatherly roles impossible. Make no mistake - a father needs to be in the home to properly and faithfully fulfill these roles.

The lack of commitment to his wife, and subsequently his children, takes God's plan for the family and perverts it from His perfect design.

Biblical fatherhood transcends biology.

This is God's design for the biblical head of household: A father is not simply a man who impregnates a woman. The father's role is that of Pastor, Provider, and Protector of the home and family unit. These roles should be embraced and lived out even before the man enters the marriage or has children. By abstaining from sex before marriage with his future wife, keeping himself pure and protecting her virtue, the man displays his understanding of God's design for marriage and demonstrates his love for his wife. And, most importantly, his obedient love of Christ, the Lord of his life.

The Christian man should begin leading his future wife in Bible study and prayer prior to marriage to help demonstrate a biblical foundation and to establish God at the center of their to be married relationship. When a Christian man takes these roles to heart early on, he honors the commands of the Lord (Ephesians 5:23-33) and establishes good habits that will shape the success of his future marriage and home. He sets the tone for the relationship, the pace for spiritual development in the home, and the foundation that will support the walls, rooms, and roof that he and his wife build together to guide and protect God's gift of children.

Conversely, any father that fails his children in one or more of the critical roles inflicts some degree of a father abandonment wound on them. When a father spiritually or physically abandons the family or significantly fails in his vital, God-set roles, he harms his wife and children and creates a vacuum that his wife cannot fill.

Despite what our culture preaches today, no matter how hard working, gifted, empowered, intelligent, "woke," or how hard a woman tries, she simply cannot effectively lead a boy into manhood.

Children require <u>both</u> parents to grow up healthy and to understand their Heavenly Father's love for them. God created children to need the polarized nurturing nature of a mother and the righteous masculinity nature of a man. And frankly, a mother's constant, throughout the day, nurturing (hugging, holding, talking, feeding, looking in the eyes, comforting, etc.) is vital in the first 6 years of child's development. This is another lie the culture is trying to persuade women about motherhood. Please do not abandoned your motherly roles.

Were this not to be the case, then God would have to be a liar.

News Flash! You're not alone – not even close!

In our sinful and corrupt world, the vast majority of men experience some type of abandonment wound from their father. Now we will consider the roles of a father and the different types of wounds created by the failure to exercise one or more of these biblical roles.

Pastor

Some men incorrectly think of pastors as only those who shepherd a church. In fact, every Christian father who serves as the spiritual leader and moral compass of the family is the pastor of the small church, his family. As a Christian man grows spiritually, his life begins to conform to Christ, loving what God loves and serving others as Christ does. As an active and present model of Christ before his family, a father needs to teach his children how to read the Scripture, how to pray, and to follow Jesus in every aspect of life. As renown Christian family and marriage counselor, Dr. James C. Dobson, guides: fathers are to tell, show, and do – every day and in every way!

Through Moses, God commanded Israel to:

> *"...love the LORD your God with all your heart and with all your soul and with all your might. And these words that I command you today shall be on your heart. You shall teach them diligently to your children, and shall talk of them when you sit in your house, and when you walk by the way, and when you lie down, and when you rise."* Deuteronomy 6:5-7 (ESV).

Being the spiritual leader is not just about taking your children to church on Sunday morning, but about how we love and follow God in every part of every day. In this, the father is not just leading spiritually but setting the moral compass of the family to reflect everything that honors God. If your father is/was not a Christian, then this component was either lacking or modeling completely in the wrong direction.

Sadly, even pastors and the most devout Christian men can fail in this area, leaving a hole in the lives of their children.

The father is to teach his children directly from the Bible and apply it to his life and theirs. We are instructed to help children memorize it or bind scripture to their hearts and minds (Deuteronomy 6:8-9). It's is the father's job to know the Lord and disciple his children. This means passing along all that Jesus taught and commanded, so that they too can repent of their sins and confess Jesus as Lord and Savior. As the father teaches children the ways of God he will know their spiritual strengths and weaknesses and can help them in their spiritual journey.

A father who does not spend the time to teach his children is a fool and will reap foolish children. (Proverbs 13).

The Pastor father prays with and for his children. He makes the time to teach his children how to pray by following our Lord's example in Matthew 6:9-13 is a good first step. This prayer reminds them that God is their Father, that how we forgive influences how we should expect God to forgive us, and it demonstrates our dependence on God for all things and rebukes our enemy the devil. The father is then to teach them to pray for others and to seek the will of God in all aspects of life.

These lessons are invaluable as they are not just words spoken to his children by actions demonstrated with and for his children. Pastoring children comes more naturally for some men than others. If you had neither a pastor-strong father nor a good example from other godly men, you might be wise to seek the help of others or utilize some of the plentiful educational resources available about effectively pastoring your children.

It is likely that your father failed to pastor you in one of the ways described above. Perhaps he failed to protect your psychological well-being by allowing others to tell lies about you or to tear you down. Maybe the failure was to not provide an example for your spiritual walk, to model what it means to follow Christ and honor God with your life. Since all men are imperfect it is likely your father failed you.

Hopefully though he was *man enough* to confess his iniquities to you and ask your forgiveness. Even if he never owned his failings, you can break the cycle by honoring God and owning your own shortcomings.

Provider

A father provides an earthly example of the love of God for His children. This is demonstrated in three key manners. The first is how a husband loves his wife. The Apostle Paul puts it this way:

> *"Husbands, love your wives, as Christ loved the church and gave himself up for her, that he might sanctify her, having cleansed her by the washing of water with the word, so that he might present the church to himself in splendor, without spot or wrinkle or any such thing, that she might be holy and without blemish. In the same way husbands should love their wives as their own bodies. He who loves his wife loves himself."* Ephesians 5:25-28 (ESV)

God loved His children so much that He gave His own Son that they might have life and be adopted into His family. Men are then commanded to show this same sacrificial love and provision for their wives. When a man gives of himself for his wife his children cannot help but take notice and work to imitate his example. In the same way, when a man refuses to marry a woman he cannot love her in this sacrificial way because he is unwilling to enter into the covenant of marriage with her under the name and accountability of God Almighty – the creator of marriage.

While having a marriage covenant does not ensure a man will give of himself this way, and he may choose to rebel against the Lord's commands, the lack of a marriage commitment in itself demonstrates his refusal to be committed and self-sacrificing. It's possible that you never experienced your father providing love for your mother on this level, in which case your father failed your mother, your siblings - and you.

The second is how a father provides love for his children.

Again, the Apostle Paul tells fathers: *"Fathers, do not provoke your children to anger, but bring them up in the discipline and instruction of the Lord."* Ephesians 6:4 (ESV). A father shows love to his children by not pushing them to the breaking point where they feel their only outlet is uncontrolled anger.

Additionally, he lovingly comes alongside them and teaches them about Christ. Often this teaching involves correcting sinful behavior and helping them to learn to replace bad behavior with actions that reflect Christ and honor God. The entire charge is for fathers to temper their instruction so as to not provoke anger through harsh discipline, poor communication, perfectionism, or his own sin - but instead to produce Godly character.

If your father was not a Christian, he would find it impossible to provide love for you in this way because you cannot teach (faith) what you do not have. Or, maybe your father professed faith in Christ but *still* failed to provide love for you in these ways.

As children grow, they often follow the example of their parents. This is especially true of boys in how they imitate the actions and words of their fathers. When a father provides a godly example of life and action his son learns what is expected of him. The boy witnesses and is likely to emulate the father's relationship with his earthly and Heavenly Father. For example, if a father realizes he was undercharged for a good or service and returns to pay what is owed, he teaches his children about honesty. Where he could have moved on, accepting the error to his benefit, he instead chose to provide his children with an example of integrity that glorifies God.

It takes very little effort for us to see the connection of our actions with the examples, or lack of examples, set by our earthly fathers.

You were watching your father navigate life and picked up all the intentional and unintentional lessons taught by his behavior and choices. And you are being watched as you walk, talk, engage others, and worship. All your good *and* bad habits are imprinting on your children – especially your son.

A father also shows love to his children through proper physical affection. Knowing that your father loved you by his hugs or kisses is an essential part of becoming a man. When a father is distant physically or is abusive rather than loving it affects us deeply as human beings. We so naturally crave attention that, especially as children, we can come to believe that even negative attention and violence comes from love, but this is a lie. Our Heavenly Father makes clear the association between love and discipline.

> *"Those whom I love I rebuke and discipline. So be earnest and repent."* Revelation 3:19 (NIV)

Love often brings discipline but should never damage a person or convince them that hatred is love or vice versa. Without positive physical acts of love, children will look to others to fulfill this need. This nearly always ends in our developing unhealthy relationships that revolve around our own needs rather than in a mutual loving relationship. A father's love for his children is vital to their growing up healthy and in the direction God intended.
Finally, a father provides for the physical needs of his children. The Apostle Paul says,

> *"But if anyone does not provide for his relatives, and especially for members of his household, he has denied the faith and is worse than an unbeliever."* 1 Timothy 5:8 (ESV)

It is the duty of a father to provide food, shelter and physical instruction for his family, but especially for his children as they are dependent on him in their weakness. If a man is unable to perform this because of a physical limitation that prevents him from working, he is still responsible for insuring provision occurs. This means caring for and managing the needs of his wife and children as well as all income and its dispersion. Not being able to work does not remove the responsibility from the man; it merely alters how he performs this task. A father is responsible for being charitable and sacrificial as well. God does not deny man his righteous passions and hobbies, but they must be pursued with greater priority placed on his care for others first.

His pleasures must not become idols in his life and cannot be given higher priority over his primary responsibilities.

A father provides instruction to his son on how to care for his body, how to overcome the obstacles of life and provides the example of how to follow Christ. Every boy will follow someone into manhood, this happens in one of three ways. One, he will blaze his own path. The boy says, "the only one who can make my dreams come true is me, so I will focus on providing the best life I can for myself."

Two, he will follow the foolish men around him. The boy will latch on to the men in his community who offer to provide him with direction, hope and purpose. This often results in his being led into manhood by criminals, gangs, extremist groups, desperate isolation, ultra-aggressive, the list goes on. Most often this path leads to jail, drug abuse, sexual exploitation and/or death.

Third, the boy will follow mom into so-called "manhood." This results in a struggle with what it means to be male and can drive a boy further away from the original plan God has for him to be a godly man and father. Obvious symptoms of this ungodly plan is the growing population of lonely, passive, effeminate or mentally confused males in their sexuality.

When a father fails to provide any of these necessary roles it directly harms his children and this failure is typically repeated by his children when they grow into adulthood.

Protector

A father will stand in ready defense of any who wish to harm his children or his family, all the while modeling for his son what it means to defend those in need and the innocent. When a father acts as a Protector he is first and foremost modeling his Heavenly Father who is,

> "...our refuge and strength, a very present help in trouble. Therefore, we will not fear though the earth gives way, though the mountains be moved into the heart of the sea, though its waters roar and foam, though the mountains tremble at its swelling." Psalm 46:1-3 (ESV)

God is the defender of all who call on His name, but also of the weak and oppressed. In the family this protection comes from the father; the more he knows the heart of God the more he imitates His ways.

The father is the natural defender of the home, providing a secure living environment. When he is absent, children live in fear/insecurity/vulnerability that the house will be broken into and that they might be harmed. A father also provides protection by teaching his children to protect themselves in his absence and to defend those weaker than themselves. As children grow, they become an extension of physical protection for themselves, their current family and their future family because of their father's instruction and example. Without the physical protection of a father in the home, children often get lured into horrific lives of destruction, including crime, sexual abuse, even slavery, and other acts of sinful behavior.

When a father fails in this way, his children too often grow up afraid or exploited.

If the man's example is one of frequent violence, then his son may grow up believing that abusing women and others is acceptable, which is in direct contrast to the nature of our Lord's instruction and example.

Children naturally develop to emotionally depend on the protection of their father. That protection reinforces that they are created in the image of God (Genesis 1:27-31) and are the most valuable part of creation. Self-worth is first built in children by the lessons and affirmation of mom and dad - and can last a lifetime. Importantly, children who grow up with low self-worth and poor self-image also struggle with seeing and believing the truth about the value God has placed on them.

They are priceless to their Heavenly Father and it is the critical role of their earthly father to express and defend that truth.

FIND YOUR FATHER SCENARIO

As men, we often don't like to talk about our pain.

Very few men want to ascribe any of their wounds to their fathers. After all, fathers are supposed to be the hero in the life of every boy. Even if our fathers were physically abusive or harmed us in a variety of other ways, in some small part of our mind we all hope that he might come back and fix the wrongs. We crave the restoration, recognition of wrongdoing, and contrition for the neglect or the traumas he inflicted. We hold out hope that he can be involved in our lives in amazing ways.

This next section is designed to help you identify your father with one or more common father-son relationship scenarios. It will help you begin to recognize the commonality we share in having some abandonment wound from our father that needs honest appraisal and forgiveness.

"My Father Died"

The trauma of losing your father travels with you for the rest of your life.

When your dad died you likely blamed God for taking him away from you. Maybe your anger at God subsided or maybe you are still holding onto it, refusing to let God "off the hook." For many men this anger at God changed over the course of time to being directed *at* their father. Maybe you remember yourself thinking, "My dad didn't have to die. He could have taken a different route to work and not died in that crash." Or, "Dad could have taken better care of himself, exercised more, gone to see the doctor for that pain, caught the cancer earlier, or could have stopped drinking." Or maybe, you struggle with why your dad chose such a dangerous profession, even elevating his desires above the vow he made to God or promises he made to you.

As your heart longed for the father that was taken away, it affected how you grew up and the man you became.

"I Never Knew My Father"

Having a father leave is terrible, but it is compounded when a boy is never able to even catch a glimpse of the man who left. For some men in this situation, your father doesn't even know you exist. The feeling you experience of being abandoned is deepened by knowing that you feel lost and your father isn't even looking for you. Your father never experienced the joy of celebrating with you in your success or consoling you in your failures. He will never meet your wife or children. There was no way for you to even conjure in your mind a scenario where your father shows up at the last minute to share in your life.

This is similar to losing a father to death, with the added complexity of having someone still "out there" to resent and be angry with. You picture scenarios of finding him in order to reconcile or to punish him for his absence, but the fantasy is dashed again and again. You build defensive walls of resentment, trying to convince yourself, "I never needed him."

"Divorce Took My Father Away"

God desires that marriage be the fundamental, honored foundation of a family – a picture of his church family, His bride.

Tragically, our culture does not share His view. Divorce is a scourge that affects the well-being of the entire family and our nation. In Chapter 2 of the book of Malachi, the Lord's hatred of divorce is explained. He hates divorce because marriage is the earthly example of God's covenant with

His people. In the same way a man and woman are joined into one person in marriage, so God's people are joined to Him. In the Old Testament this was illustrated by the Lord's relationship with Israel. In the New Testament, it is Christians who become one with Jesus Christ. Ephesians 5:22-33 (ESV).

As a Believer, we would never want Christ to abandon His covenantal commitment to us. Similarly, men, we should never abandon the commitment to our wife.

In the Bible, there is truly no support or excuse for divorce that does not negatively affect souls and lives. Divorce is evidence of a hardness of heart or a poor decision in a spouse, and is detestable to God. Matthew 19:8-9 (ESV). In areas of conflict with our spouse, the Bible would direct that we extend forgiveness to her and seek her betterment over our own. Frankly speaking, what women would not love to be in a marriage when her husband is loving her as Christ loved the church?

Sadly, non-Christians know little of God's desire to have marriage kept pure and the self-sacrifice the commitment requires from those involved. Even many Christians choose to openly disobey God's command, leading to their sin that destroys the family. Even though your mom and dad got divorced and your dad left, it wasn't your fault.

But, make no mistake, there are ALWAYS consequences to the soul. God is not a liar.

With divorce and the splitting of a family cup, here are some common scenarios that the children face as a result.

"I Competed with Dad's 'New' Family"

Your dad felt obligated to pick you up, but you spent more time with his new wife and kids than him. Instead of feeling like your dad wanted you to be around all the time, you felt that you were a second-class citizen in his life. His new children took precedence and you were factored in based on a sense of obligation, not his desire personally to be with you or only by a court order.

"I Had No Dad"

Because of the divorce, your dad left the home and never showed back up in your life.

Maybe he resurfaced in your adult years, claiming that he tried to be involved but your mom kept him out. You are left wondering how hard he tried, feeling that if he truly wanted a relationship with you, he could have been creative and committed to doing all he could to prove that to you someday. He could have written you a letter each day telling you how much he missed and loved you. He could have kept a copy of each letter so that even if your mom didn't give you the letters, when you turned 18-years old he could have hand-delivered these letters to you. But he didn't do this or make any other adaptive gesture to prove his love. He was just gone and all talk – no sacrificial action.

"My Father Was in Jail"

Some men's fathers were locked up when they were growing up. Seeing dad meant going to the jail or prison and having limited interaction. You lived with that fear and shame forged by this identity. Your father was never able to take you outside, play catch, go the movies or put you to bed. Other fatherless boys first came to know their father when they too were locked up with him in the prison system. Maybe you felt the sins of your father were part of your DNA and you were destined to go to jail because that is where your father was. All you know is the bad about your father.

"Seeing My Father Was A Sporadic Event"

Your father saw you on the weekend, every other week, a few days a month, or maybe only a few days or weeks every year. Your heart wanted to see your father every day - to know he was there for you and to have the comfort and security of his consistent presence. What you received was a man who tried to cram a year of life into a few days and then couldn't figure out why you were so upset at everything he did. You wondered why he didn't care more. Why didn't dad's heart have a hole in the shape of you? Why didn't he invest in you? Did your achievements matter? Was he proud of you, even though he was remote?

The physical distance destroyed your potential emotional closeness, and ripped open the scab of being fatherless – time and time again.

"My Father Lived in Our Home, I Think..."

Your father worked long hours, multiple jobs or both. You occasionally saw him, but he was so consumed with life outside of the house that he seemed to be more of a ghost than an actual person. He provided a roof over your head, clothes on your back and food in your stomach but not much else. Maybe he would come home from work, eat dinner and then go straight into his home office only to emerge long after you went to bed. His absence in your life was significant and felt deeply, but you could never claim he abandoned you because he was there living in your house. For you, dad being present but not "there for you" seemed like an even greater insult because he saw you, but you still felt invisible.

His passive role in your life was active rejection. His silence spoke volumes. You ranked somewhere below anything else of importance in his life.

"My Father was Always Drunk or Drugged Out"

Coming home and knowing your father will be drunk or drugged out is a terrifying situation for anyone, but when this man is your example of manhood it deepens the hurt. How can he protect you? How can he pastor or provide for you? This situation also led to your father being unreliable, an embarrassment and violent. Maybe he told you he would pick you up after school, only to leave you waiting for hours. You could walk home or catch a ride with a friend, but you knew that doing this would cause violent outbursts when he did show up to find you not where he told you to be.

Your father didn't abandon you physically, but he was gone all the same. He abandoned you spiritually.

You came to associate the strongest of negative emotions in relation to your dad: shame, embarrassment, fear, disgust, and pity. You couldn't make sense of his weakness or choices. Why was he so miserable? Why is he so weak? Why did he love a drug more than me, his family? What is it about you and your family that was so horrific that he felt the overwhelming need to escape it?

You wondered if that was your destiny too. Is this natural and just how men deal with life, family, and challenges?

"My Dad Was an Armchair Quarterback"

You were an element of your dad's life, but not a treasured priority. You learned to play his game and understood the terms of engagement that caused the least friction or correction. Upon returning home from work or wherever he was all day your father retired to his easy chair. To engage him in conversation required you to wait for a commercial break or a stopping point in his book or other distraction. You stood there waiting quietly for an opening to ask a question, knowing you needed to be clear and concise with your inquiry or risk being yelled at. The vast majority of fatherly interaction was like this, leaving you wondering what it meant to be a father - or a man for that matter. Why was this so difficult?

Society tried to convince you that small amounts of attention and "quality time," was more important than the quantity of time together, but you know that for the lie it is. Even lack-luster time spent with you would have demonstrated that he loved you enough to sacrifice his agenda to be with you. You had fantasies and brief glimpses of what your relationship could have been like if you'd been more special to dad.
You learned a warped lesson that family and children have a place in a man's life, but that place is behind many other things which matter more to him.

"My Father Hated Me"

It might seem cliché but there is truth in the saying, "the opposite of love is indifference."

Being allowed to do what is harmful or not caring enough to be deeply connected to him, especially toward a son, doesn't demonstrate love. Indifference robbed you of the kind words and gentle touches from your father that you desperately wanted and needed. This left you wondering what was so wrong with you that you deserved to be treated with such hatred? In response, at first you worked hard to change what seemed so confusing and offensive, but eventually you gave up trying to be seen and appreciated. Perhaps you rebelled as much as possible for attention.

The feelings of worthlessness and undesirability ran your life and affected how your treated others.

"My Dad Married A Feminist or an Over-bearing Women"

God's design for men in the home is to be the Pastor, Provider, and Protector that He ordained them to be. This biblical man is also the spiritual head of the home, demonstrating and modeling positive masculinity and leadership. His wife and children support, respect, and submit to him and his authority in this role.

Whether he knew it or not, *your* dad married a feminist, perhaps because of his own inherent weakness, passivity, and shortcomings most likely caused by his lack of a good father in his life. Typically, a feminist will demonstrate the dominance to try to assume the headship of the household. Therefore, because of your mom's aggressiveness, or because your dad simply wasn't around, your mom wore the pants and "was the man" in the home.

In his void, your mom adopted masculine traits that were both unbalanced and unnatural in the family dynamic. She emasculated your father through critique and open challenge in front of you. Time and time again, he gave up his rightful position and responsibility of head of household.

You may even have been caught in the middle between your mother and father, as she put additional love and unwanted attention on you while her affection waned for your deficient dad, creating a competitive tension between you. Or, through her unhealthy coddling, over-bearing attention by doing most everything for you destroyed your confidence. This damages motivation and signals to a boy's soul, "she must not think I can do it or have what it takes". As a result, you shrunk back in your natural masculine, risk-taking tendencies, and became fearful of leaving the home nest to take on and conquer your own path.

You don't know what a biblical marriage looks like or how men and women in a godly home interact and raise healthy children because you've never seen it.

ALL WOUNDS ARE PAINFUL

No matter what type of abandonment wound or father wounds you've suffered from, please understand that they are all do significant damage.

As men, we often manipulate our memory of the past to help us cope with or ignore the hurts we suffered. It's a powerful and natural defense mechanism to square up some of the accounts that continue to feel indebted. Going back to that pain seems fruitless to you so, (consciously or unconsciously), you decide to "let it go". But it festers. You might be the guy who says, "My dad wasn't really that bad. Sure, he did *this* or didn't do *that*, but none of us are perfect." You might feel like you're giving grace and being Christian-like in this way.

However, by downplaying the hurt and removing the responsibility of your father for his actions it perpetuates your covering up the pain. This response does not help heal your wounds - it merely serves as fertile ground for unforgiveness.

By not authentically dealing with the issues as they truly are, you might feel there is no need to forgive your father.

Straight Talk for Men

In order for you to once-and-for-all face the truth, confront the facts, forgive, and to heal you will have to have the courage through this process to open yourself back up to those hurts. Be *man enough* to face the truth.

Maybe you are the guy who says, "No one can understand how terrible my father was and the living hell he put me through. You'd hate him too." You are correct that the majority of other people cannot understand the exact depth of your pain. But that does not make your experience worse than that of another man. Every wound needs to be honestly evaluated, worked through and then forgiveness extended.

Why is forgiveness a central pillar to your relationship with Jesus Christ?

Forgiving your father for his falling woefully short in his fatherhood responsibilities and the way it has wounded you <u>does not excuse his behavior and may never end in reconciliation</u>, but it does recognize and respond to God's call on us to biblical forgiveness.

> *"For while we were still weak, at the right time Christ died for the ungodly. For one will scarcely die for a righteous person- though perhaps for a good person one would dare even to die-but God shows his love for us in that while we were still sinners, Christ died for us. Since, therefore, we have now been justified by his blood, much more shall we be saved by him from the wrath of God. For if while we were enemies we were reconciled to God by the death of his Son, much more, now that we are reconciled, shall we be saved by his life."*
> Romans 5:6-10 (ESV)

In the same way that, though we were still his enemies, Christ forgave us, He calls us to forgive others. Biblical forgiveness requires you to identify the sin for what it is and then specifically forgive the offender for that particular sin as you would have God forgive you for your sin.
Isn't just "granting grace" or "moving on" enough? No!

It's not enough to have adapted to the reality of the pain and wounds you have faced; to have lowered your expectations; to let it slide; to have struggled to find your own way and own worth; or to secretly hold on to that poor fatherly example as an easy excuse for your own bad behavior. It is not enough to look the other way and to build lifelong defense strategies to counteract the pain. It's not enough to try to forget.

We must, for our own good and for the sake of our eternal souls, forgive.

Is that easier said than done? Yes. But let me ask you this, men. Do you just seek an easy life? Is that what being a man, especially a Christian man, is all about? Is comfort and ease the fuel for warrior men? For Pastors, Providers and Protectors? Of course not.

My brother - hear me now. I promise you this: Working through this pain in the journey to authentic and lasting forgiveness will be a struggle, **but it will be worth it in the end**. Not doing this is like having a festering wound that you refuse to acknowledge or address with the medical attention it requires.

Are you going to allow your wound to continue to fester inside of you?

Are you going to pass the wound down generationally?

Or - will you obey God, and through the power of the Holy Spirit forgive your father so the wound can begin to heal?

| Chapter 3: Study |

MAN UP!

Let's get rolling. This is a chance for you to start working through your wound. I encourage and challenge you to be open and fully honest with yourself. This painful process may dredge up old hurts that you would rather forget than to deal with, but the path to healing requires you to evaluate them.

Write down your answers in an electronic document or a journal so that you can refer back to them later as you begin to write your *Forgiveness Letter*.

NEXT STEPS: Working through the chapter

    a. If your father abandoned you, how old where you when he left?

    b. If your father was around but abandoned his biblical roles, when did you first notice his lack of intentionality in your life?

c. My Father was: use the list above to identify your father (he may fit several categories).

d. In what ways did you father fail to provide for you?

e. In what ways did he fail to protect you?

f. I wish my dad had pastored (spiritually led/fed) me in these ways:

g. What feelings came up while you were working through the above questions?

GET ROLLING with the <u>Companion Guide</u>: Preparation to write a *Forgiveness Letter*:

- Utilize the *Man Enough to Forgive* Personal Study Journal workbook

| Scripture References |

1. Be humble. Philippians 2:3 (NASB)

2. Apostle Paul instructs on how men should love their wives. Ephesians 5:25-28 (ESV)

3. Apostle Paul tells men to raise children with discipline and instruction in the Lord. Ephesians 6:4 (ESV)

4. The Lord disciplines those He loves. Hebrews 12:4-11 (NIV)

5. Men are to provide for the needs of his children. 1 Timothy 5:8 (ESV)

6. The Lord is our refuge and strength. Psalm 46:1-3 (ESV)

7. Children are created in the image of God. Genesis 1:27-31 (NASB)

8. We must teach children to love the Lord. Deuteronomy 6:5-7 (ESV)

9. A man who doesn't teach his children will reap foolish children. Proverbs 13 (NASB)

10. Teach children to pray The Lord's Prayer. Matthew 6:9-13 (NASB)

11. Christian believers become one with Christ. Ephesians 5:22-33 (NASB)

12. God detests divorce. Matthew 19:8-9 (NASB)

13. Because we have been forgiven, we must forgive. Romans 5:6-10 (ESV)

The Battle for the Truth

SERIES TWO

There is Absolute Truth
Seek It!

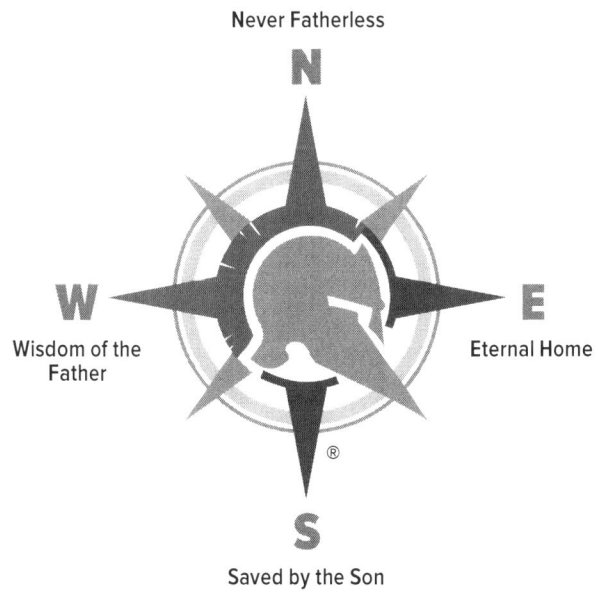

mercy

[mer·cy] **noun**

The aspect of God's love that causes Him to help the miserable, just as grace, is the aspect of His love that moves Him to forgive the guilty.

CHAPTER FOUR

The Lies of Fatherlessness

"Be on the alert, stand firm in the faith, act like men, be strong."
1 Corinthians 16:13 (NASB)

| Quick Start |

Every man must take responsibility for his own actions. Your father's failures are his personal responsibility, just as your failings are yours. Unfortunately, as your role model of manhood and biblical fatherhood your father's failings have impacted your life significantly. As you begin the journey of forgiving your father for failing you, it is vital that we uncover the lies you came to believe because you were fatherless.

Again, if your father did not fulfill his biblical roles of Pastor, Provider, and Protector *you have a fatherless wound*. If not, God is a liar.

The Hard Truth

Since we live in a broken world, tainted by sin and corruption, we can trace back our deepest wounds to the sinful actions of ourselves and others. The key is to recognize who needs to own the responsibility for that sin and how to reconcile with God in Christ. Your father's own sinful selfish desires are what caused him to abandon you and fail in his sacred responsibility as father. God calls men to lead and care for their children but *your* father chose instead to abandon these responsibilities. As a result of this sin, he did not value you as an important and impressionable soul, he didn't rescue you, and wasn't a part of your life in all of the other ways God has commanded men to lead and provide for their children.

Like with us all, sin at its root is responsible for all of your hurt, pain, confusion, troubles, loneliness, sadness, and anger.

Along with this brokenness came lies that you learned to accept about yourself in relation to your father. You deceived yourself with some untruths, still others were told to you. But a lie is a lie, no matter the source. You might have believed that it was your fault that your father left; that you were better off without him; that you can fix the problem yourself and just "man-up"; that your negative behavior is forever your father's fault; or a myriad of other lies. The *truth* is your father's sinful heart drove him to abandon you and he is responsible for that - not you. However, the choices you made and are making today, in the aftermath of his sin, are your responsibility. Often, when we have been truly sinned against, it is in our sin, we have responded in sinful ways. You need to be willing to own them if you wish to begin to heal from your abandonment wound.

Men's response to significant life crisis tends to be one of two reactions: fight or flight. And let's be real here – a father abandoning his son qualifies as crisis! Your natural reaction to being abandoned may have been to work yourself like crazy to try and win or earn your fathers love - the *fight* response. Or you may have attempted to escape your pain and the related emotional turmoil by rebelling against everything and everyone - the *flight* response. You might have even tried both approaches, fighting at times, and flying away at others.

Whether you fought the pain, ran from it, or were simply lost and paralyzed by the deep-seated disconnect between what *was* versus how life *should* be, your style of reaction impacted the behavioral choices you made and influenced how the lies of abandonment manifest in your life.

Today, you need to understand the connection between your abandonment and your behavior, based on the lies you believed so you can begin to heal. As the Holy Spirit reveals these connections to you, you must have the courage to accept it as truth. You cannot successfully "fake this until you make it" with this key step. Pushing it aside does not make it go away. If your lack of forgiveness persists, your hurt will continue to inform and control your life in negative and unhealthy manners.

Unforgiveness is sin for which you will need to repent and ask God to forgive you, so you can become the man God intended by His strength.

| Road Map |

THE LIES YOU BELIEVED

Your father's failures are his personal responsibility, just as your failings are your own. As your role model of manhood and fatherhood, your father's failings have impacted you deeply. As you begin the journey of forgiving your father for failing you, it is vital that we uncover the lies you came to believe because you were fatherless. I will outline the big picture and then help you better identify and understand how lies you believed set the course for the negative impact that followed.

We live in a broken world because of sin. God created the world and intentionally placed humanity in it as the pinnacle of His creation. In Genesis 1:26 (NASB) we read,

> "Then God said, 'Let Us make man in Our image, according to Our likeness; and let them rule over the fish of the sea and over the birds of the sky and over the cattle and over all the earth, and over every creeping thing that creeps on the earth.'"

We were created in the image of God, designed to be in relationship with our Heavenly Father. Humans were meant to bring God glory in all that we say and do, but our sin prevents us from glorifying and worshiping God as He deserves.

When Adam disobeyed God's command to not eat fruit from the Tree of the Knowledge of Good and Evil, sin then entered the world and brought death and corruption. At its core, sin is disobedience of the commands of God. Sin drives us away from the worship and glorification of God and towards selfishness and a desire to make ourselves our own god.

This might sound harsh, but it is the truth. Your father abandoned you because of his own sinful selfish desires.

His sin led him to not value you as he should, not to rescue you, and to not be a part of your life in all of the other ways God has meant men to lead and provide for their children. Sin is the foundation of all of your hurt, pain, confusion, troubles, loneliness, sadness and anger.

Where God calls men to lead and care for their children your father chose instead to fail in these biblical responsibilities, thus abandoning you.

All of this is terrible and matters greatly in your life. There's encouraging news though! Here forward you can *choose* freedom. You can decide not to wallow and submit to the addiction of that pain. You can reject the premise that your father's abandonment will continue to be a catalyst that drives your life.

Next, I'll make some generalizations and representative statements regarding experiences and emotions that many men felt as boys and may have continued into manhood. This isn't to be melodramatic or to suggest they are exactly how you feel. However, I predict that you'll likely find more truth in the characterizations than not.

The following is a list of lies you potentially believed in relation to your father's sinful actions. You will likely recognize and identify with one or more of these as being part of your story.

Or, as you work through this you may come to terms with *additional* lies that you were fed and accepted as truth. Your view of your father often finds its root in the lies you believed. In order to cope, without the maturity, guidance and modeling from a Christian man in the home, you were likely either in denial and ignored your father's failure while issuing undue praise for him or, more likely, you had extremely negative associations with your dad. This soul trauma is inevitable.

Lie #1: It's My Fault That Dad Left.

The pain you felt every day that your dad was gone was fueled by feelings of confusion and anger.

Due to the natural desire to defend your would-be "hero," you felt you had to suppress the anger so that you could still love him. Deep down you believed your love would bring your father back home. As a child, you examined your own simple shortcomings in order to absolve his guilt by blaming yourself. Maybe dad left because of all the times you didn't clean your room or eat your vegetables. Maybe he split because you earned poor grades. Perhaps it was because he didn't like how you looked or the music you listened to. It could have been because he hated your friends, or a million other disconnected reasons that you included in a narrative to support your immature thoughts that "if only I had (fill in the blank here) then dad would have stayed." You tried to fix some of the things that you blamed yourself for, hoping he would see the change and that your hero would return.

Passing along the blame, it is possible that your mother, siblings or others told you it was your fault that your father left.

This too is a lie. Your father chose to leave, to be selfish, and to give in to the sin of abandonment – forsaking his fatherhood roles.

You are not and were not to blame for him leaving you and there's no need to carry that debilitating belief forward.

Chances are that as time passed this blame turned into anger and hatred for your dad. Maybe that hate still lingers, and perhaps it's still white hot. However, with this new and clear perspective take the time now to unburden yourself. It may feel awkward to formally let this go but trust me, it allows the Holy Spirit to work in you.

Say it with me now. "My father left. It was his choice and it was not my fault. I will no longer accept blame that was not mine. I will let my father own the consequences for his own sin."

Lie #2: I Don't Need a Father. I Was/Am Better Off With Him Gone.

"I don't need that jerk around! All he ever did was cause problems and I am glad he is gone. I am better off without him!" You made statement like these or similar ones with even harsher language. When pressed by others about your dad being absent, all of the negative emotions came flooding out with anger and hatred at the front of the line. With every passing year this lie became stronger and became more real.

Maybe you learned this lie from your mother and others around you. In their desire to help you cope with the loss, they told you this lie to try and ease the pain. You are better off without him.

No matter how this lie was presented in your life, it is still a lie. We've covered the biblical jobs of a father. You needed him to perform his role so that you could grow into manhood. Yes, he failed you and you survived anyway, but it doesn't remove the fact that you needed him in your life. Right now you might be thinking, "Yes, but my dad was abusive. I lived in fear, so it's not a lie. I was better off with him gone." Certainly, the abuse you suffered is terrible. I am not asking you to let your father off the hook for his sinful actions towards you and your family. In this circumstance, you may indeed have been more physically safe with your father gone. That does not change the fact that God meant for boys to be led and protected by our fathers. His absence robbed you of that.

It is important to realize and to faithfully understand that "better off" does not mean "well".

You needed him to be the man God called him to be - and he failed.

Lie #3: I Just Need To "Suck It Up" and "Get Over It."

The loss due to your father's absence was a constant ache in your soul. It almost felt like a living parasite that fed off memories and burrowed deeper in your flesh when you saw other happy boys with their fathers. Maybe you used drugs, alcohol, or jumped around from woman to woman to mask the pain.

Or perhaps you went to individual counseling or group therapy - or tried countless other approaches to compensate and get over the hurt. You kept telling yourself that you just need to "suck it up" or "forgive and forget" to move beyond the pain, but you couldn't. After all, you were told that "big boys don't cry" or show emotions.

This is a lie that we probably *still* tell ourselves so that we don't have deal with the emotions of the abandonment wound. Hear me on this, my brother. This isn't something you just wash off your hands and then go on with life. It requires deep and courageous honesty with yourself, with the Lord, and ultimately directly with your father in the *Forgiveness Letter* you'll write to him.

Lie #4: Dad's Absence Didn't Negatively Impact My Life or My Choices.

Dad was gone, but mom tried to pick up his slack and fill-in where he left off. She made sure I did my homework, that I was active in sports, and that I participated in Boy Scouts and clubs and so many other things. Sure, it would have been *nice* for my dad to be there to support and cheer for me, but I really didn't notice his absence. Other people helped teach me to navigate life milestones like learning to drive, preparing for college, getting a job, and knowing how to live independently. God provided lots of people to fill the void, so I shouldn't complain.

For many, friends filled the void left by the father and were key influencers in life choices. If that is you, then you likely stood before a judge in municipal court at least once, maybe more often, and did some time in juvenile detention or jail. Perhaps you lived on the streets or were homeless, surfing from one friend's couch to another. Life was one poor choice after another that if you looked back on it now, too many choices were made by others *for* you. You just went along for the ride.

No matter what this looked like for you, it is a lie is that your dad's absence had no effect on you. Clearly it did.

We live in a feminized culture that belittles men, portraying them to be largely incompetent, dumb and primal animals. It then offers to swap these weak men with stronger women, propagandizing that this is an acceptable and favorable substitute for men and their role in the home or even in the church. It was not and it is not. Only a man can sufficiently model and cultivate biblical masculinity in a boy. Young men raised by women will miss some critical components of becoming a man of God due to the deficiencies of that experience that are directly counter to Creator God's design.

Your father's absence robbed you of genuine manhood training. He wasn't there to provide direction, to pastor you through life, or to protect you from those who sought to exploit you. His absence affected your life in countless ways. In order to begin healing you need to acknowledge this as fact. Because I desperately want you to experience the full healing that is 100% available to you now, we must face into these hard truths.

Lie #5: I Am Not Responsible for My Actions. They are Dad's Fault.

"If my dad had stayed then I would never have hung out with the guys who got me into trouble or been hooked on drugs. My dad wouldn't have allowed me to hang out with those people. When I beat my girlfriend or my wife, it was because I learned to mistreat women by watching him. I would never have been promiscuous and sexually irresponsible, getting those girls pregnant or encouraged their abortions. I wouldn't have abandoned my own children. In fact, all the terrible things that have happened are *his* fault."

You might feel that *everything* bad that happened would have been prevented if your dad had been in your life. To some extent you may be right.

If he was the Pastor, Provider, and Protector he should have been, he might very well have saved you from much pain and heartache. Then again, even dads that are present in the home fail in some important ways. No matter, you are responsible for the life choices you made, for your behavior, and you own the consequences. When your buddies asked you to go shoplift or vandalize the local minimart, you could have said "no." Or you decided to have sex outside of the marriage covenant that resulted in a child that was murdered in the womb.

In the same way that your heart longs for your father to take responsibility for his mistakes in your life, you have to own your mistakes.

Lie #6: It's Impossible to Trust Other People.

When your dad left, you experienced broken promise after broken promise from him or others. From your mom's boyfriends who made promises only to break them after they began sleeping with your mother or after they broke up and he left too. Understand that this is a *second, or third, etc.* abandonment.

Depending on how long he was in the home, your age at the time, and how close you became, maybe this even created a second meaningful fatherless wound that will need to be acknowledged and forgiven. Every man who made promises and forged a relationship with you has the potential of creating another wound. These wounds are like the calluses that you get on your hands from months of hard labor. Your heart forms similar calluses when promises are made and broken. Maybe they were from family members or men in the community who promised to teach you or take you places - only to cancel on you, leaving you wondering who you can trust.

Men who do not keep their word, break their promises is the opposite of the Heavenly Father. I still witness men who do this regularly, and pretend this behavior is no big deal.

God is not a liar.

Broken promises lead to a deep belief that we have little or no value, but that is a lie. Your value and worth do not come from the validation of others, but from God. He created you in His image, making you immeasurably important to Him. Our Heavenly Father didn't stop there. He became incarnate in Jesus Christ to *save you* from sin and death, adopting you into a new permanent family. Your brothers and sisters in Christ will still fail you from time to time, but your Heavenly Father and Savior will never fail you and can always be trusted. God will never leave and never forsake you. The Bible tells us He is,

"A father to the fatherless, a defender of widows, is God in his holy dwelling." Psalm 68:5 (NIV)

Lie #7: I Will Always Be Broken. Nothing Can Heal Me.

Your father leaving you was wrong and will matter significantly in your life, but it is not who you are. The brokenness you feel is real – but it is lie is that you can never heal. In Christ, you can.

The road to restoration can be long, but with the help of the Holy Spirit <u>you will make it</u>. As you progress through *Man Enough to Forgive* I will walk with you to begin this process. It requires you to do the self-work and to firmly reject the lie that you cannot and will not get past this. Remain hopeful that, through Christ and His forgiveness, you can be the man God created you to be.

FIGHT OR FLIGHT

Considering these common lies often causes the feelings that you experienced growing up to resurface. Reliving the pain, anger, and sorrow is never easy but it will allow you to evaluate your response to these lies. Our most ingrained survival instincts, fight or flight, are triggered in the face of challenges and tough times.

More often than not when the fight or flight response kicked in you chose to either try to earn (fight for) your father's love or rebel (flight from) the situation and those challenging emotions.

Lie #8: I am Successful – Perfection is Good.

Statistically, less than 15% of fatherless boys choose to fight for their father's affection and love.

This fight is usually an indirect battle with the father, in that the boy engages in a never-ending pursuit of perfection and has an obsessive desire to win at everything. This can manifest in the willingness to take dangerous risks or a drive to accomplish attention-getting feats in an effort to encourage your father's return and affection or to prove your worth.

Maybe you strove to excel at sports to the point where you sacrificed your body. Or maybe you started your own business, working tirelessly to get rich and powerful. It could be the pursuit of any number of job titles, awards, or things that you felt you needed to prove your value. Subsequently you placed more value in that *than* your family. In all of this, you were willing to risk life and limb for your father's attention to convince him you were worthy of his time and love. Many, many "successful" men, including Presidents of the United States fit into this category. They set their sights on the future and refuse to allow others to stand in their way, while secretly being motivated by the need to overcome issues of self-worth and earn public affirmation to fill the hole in their heart left by their absent father.

Most fatherless boys react in open rebellion, to flee, because of the anger one felt given the wounds of fatherhood abandonment and/or indifference.

This rebellion could take a variety of emotional forms: angry aggression, self-loathing, sadness, isolation and acting out against authority. This is why 85% of fatherless boys get into so much trouble and continue the cycle of destructive behavior and abandonment. Your rebellion caused more problems than it solved. In truth, it was an ineffective approach at escaping the pain and the lies you believed when your father left.

Open your eyes. Recognize all of the symptoms and destruction the fatherless create in the next generation of families, the churches, the communities, and the nation.

It is quite possible that you both fought *and* ran in an endless course correction creating constant instability. Both of these approaches violate the system God designed for the family and the role men play in that system. Men are called to place the welfare of their spouse and children above one's own selfish ambitions, caring for them as Christ cares for the Church. We know that it a tall order, but you need to be honest about both your father's failing and how you've responded to that biblical mandate, so that you can begin to heal from your wound.

With the direct support of the Holy Spirit, you *can* take responsibility for any actions that resulted from your choices and begin the steps of restoration.

Chapter 4: Study

As a reminder, this section is designed to help you work through the healing process. It requires an open and honest heart that desires to experience the healing of God. We encourage that you write down your answers in an electronic document or a journal so that you can refer back to them later as you begin to write your **Forgiveness Letter**.

NEXT STEPS: Working through the chapter

a. Write a list of the lies you came to believe. If there are additional lies that had great negative impact, record those too.

b. What specific ways did those lies influence your choices as a child? How about as an adult?

c. These lies are harmful. The first step to disarming them is to admit that you cannot work your way out of the darkness alone. You need Christ's help. What is keeping you from asking Jesus to help you stop believing the lies?

d. Which crisis response, fight or flight, do you think best describes your behavior?

e. How did your response help to feed the lies you believed?

f. How did your fight or flight reaction perpetuate and give power to the lie (a self-fulfilling prophesy)?

GET ROLLING with the <u>Companion Guide</u>: Preparation to write a *Forgiveness Letter*:

- Utilize the *Man Enough to Forgive* Personal Study Journal workbook

| Scripture References |

1. Be firm in faith, be strong, and act like men. 1 Corinthians 16:13 (NASB)

2. Man is created in God's image. Genesis 1:26 (NASB)

3. God is a father to the fatherless. Psalm 68:5 (NIV)

adoption

[adop·tion] **noun**

A new creature, born again into a new family. Selection as a son endows him with the status and privileges of the family.

CHAPTER FIVE

The Truth about How My Heavenly Father Sees Me

"Brothers, do not be children in your thinking.
Be infants in evil, but in your thinking be mature."
1 Corinthians 14:20 (ESV)

| Quick Start |

"Where were you God? How could you let me suffer like this?"

These questions represent just two of the countless questions and hours you spent as a boy asking how a loving, merciful God could allow terrible pain and suffering in the lives of children. As a Christian man, you know that there must be more to the question than this, but it is so hard to reconcile suffering with God's love for His children. In the face of your pain, simply being told that "God turns suffering into blessing for those who love him" seems like a platitude. It may feel like you're letting God off the hook for not doing anything in your times of need.

The truth is that God's creation was perfect until Adam chose to be disobedient and welcomed death and corruption into the world.

Ultimately, the suffering we experience is a descendant of both our sin and the sin of others. As a result, we must struggle through a world that is being torn apart by corruption. By contrast, God's love for His people provides countless blessings for humanity through His general grace. He even sacrificed His own Son for the salvation of His children, not because He owed us anything but because of His great love for His people. Christ suffered *for* us then.

Even now He suffers *with* us as we are joined to Him in the Church (the body of Christ).

Rather than blaming God for the terrible sufferings we have endured because of sin and corruption we should be focusing on who we are in Christ Jesus. Believers are the adopted children of our Heavenly Father and are brothers with Christ. Jesus is the Son of God by nature in that He is eternally both God and His Son. We too are made sons of God by our connection to Jesus. The Son reveals to us the nature and character of the Father and His life demonstrates how the sons of God are to live in the midst of a corrupt and sinful world that is not our home.

In short, we are called to a live life as close to Jesus' as possible. When God looks at us, He doesn't see our flaws - He sees Jesus.

"Are you calling me a liar?"

As you fully receive this calling, you can no longer live in the lies of the past. Holding on to those lies essentially endorses them as true.

In other words, you're calling God a liar. <u>God alone declares the truth about you</u>.

When you repent for your sins, He deems them forgiven forever and He anoints you a worthy saint in Jesus Christ alone. What an incredible affirmation! Let me say it another profound way. You are *perfect* in Christ. You have a new identity in Him. To remain in this state of renewed fellowship with your Heavenly Father, we must repent each day when we live out the lies of the past or any current sins. You must proactively replace the old lies with the truth from God's Word. Your emotions/feelings get trumped by God's clear declarations on how He now sees you.

Knowing this truth is not enough. You must genuinely believe this truth. Believing the truth requires you to change how you live. If you believe your Heavenly Father has forgiven and adopted you, then you will imitate Him by forgiving your earthly father. True forgiveness means not dwelling on the hurt or the lies that came from your pain, but once and for all, putting it in the past and maturing in Christ.

It is the difference between a scar and an open wound. An open-wound needs to be cleaned, closed, and allowed to heal. If you pick at a wound while it is still healing, it will fester and grow worse. Once healed though, a bumped scar may still hurt but it won't fully open up and become infected as it did in the past.

Our scars are part of us, but the Lord loves us *with our scars*.

| Road Map |

WHY DID GOD ALLOW THIS TO HAPPEN?

Looking back on your father wounds, you sometimes find yourself wondering why God allowed you to suffer at all. After all, He *is* love, right!?! So how can a loving and merciful God allow terrible pain and suffering in the lives of children?

The answer goes back to the beginning of all creation.

What God originally created was perfect and *without* suffering, (Genesis 1), but Adam chose disobedience rather than righteousness and sin entered the world (Genesis 3). Sin ushered in corruption and death to the world and with it came suffering for all humanity (Romans 5:12-21; 2 Peter 2:19). The Bible tells us that we have all sinned and earned the punishment of death (Romans 3:23; 6:23). For those of us saved by Christ, suffering does not end because suffering is part of the corrupted character of the world and those in it.

This persecution does not stop for Christians. In fact, if we are obedient to God and live in a Christ-like matter, righteous suffering will come because the world will hate us as it hated Him (Matthew 10:22; John 15:18). God is Sovereign and uses all things, all events, and even hardship, heartache, and evil to shape us to be more like Him. All to bring Him glory that only He deserves. A wonderful verse to meditate on is Isaiah 45. We must learn to prefer God's ways and God's glory above all else.

The Blame Game

We often lose our perspective about the source of our suffering, choosing instead to blame our Heavenly Father for what we perceive as His apathy and indifference. What we should never forget is that He loved us so much that He sent His only Son to save us from the corruption and death that we, humanity, caused and perpetrated in the world (1 John 4:9-10). We also know that He has never abandoned His precious children. Those who are Saved in Christ have received the Holy Spirit to guide, to guard, and as a guarantor of salvation (Matthew 13:1-11; Romans 5:3-5; Hebrews 10:12-23).

Suffering is never easy. Because God loves us He *uses* our suffering to refine us as believers and develop in us a more Christ-like character. This is why the Apostle Paul says,

> *"And we know that for those who love God all things work together for good, for those who are called according to his purpose."* Romans 8:28 (NASB)

This is not to say God causes suffering, but that He can take suffering and turn it into blessings for His Children. We suffer because of sin, but our Heavenly Father turns evil into blessing for us just as He did for Joseph, the son of Jacob, in the Book of Genesis.

HOW OUR HEAVENLY FATHER SEES US

Christians are the adopted children of our Heavenly Father and brothers with Christ. Jesus is the Son of God from eternity past and became man through the virgin Mary. He is eternally both God and Son, whereas we are *made* sons of God by our connection to the Father through Jesus. There is no adoption opportunity apart from the incarnate Christ because,

> *"...no one knows the Son except the Father, and no one knows the Father except the Son and anyone to whom the Son chooses to reveal him."* Matthew 11:27 (NASB)

The Son reveals to us the nature and character of the Father. Jesus' life demonstrates how sons of God (you and I) are to live in the midst of a corrupt and sinful world. Our adoption as sons is a demonstration of the elective grace of God. This is incredibly important for us to understand so that it can inform our perspective and affect how we live.

God sees the sin and disobedience of those who have <u>not</u> believed and trust their faith in Christ for salvation. Alternately, in those who believe, He sees the righteousness of Christ and thus views them as sons.

> *"But when the fullness of time had come, God sent forth his Son, born of woman, born under the law, to redeem those who were under the law, so that we might receive adoption as sons."* Galatians 4:4-5 (NASB)

As the adopted sons of God, we are redeemed from the punishment of the law, through Christ. God no longer sees us as guilty, rather righteous,

> *"in him we have redemption through his blood, the forgiveness of our trespasses, according to the riches of his grace."* Ephesians 1:7 (NASB)

Paul goes on to explain that,

> *"And because you are sons, God has sent the Spirit of his Son into our hearts, crying, 'Abba! Father!' So you are no longer a slave, but a son, and if a son, then an heir through God."* (Galatians 4:6-7).

Not only does our Heavenly Father see the Son in us, but He has given us the Holy Spirit as well. In addition to the eternal Son becoming man to save us from sin and corruption, the Father also provided us with the eternal Holy Spirit that we might become His adopted sons. What amazing gifts! **Though your earthly father failed you, your Heavenly Father continues to give you grace and mercy**. Our slavery to sin is gone and the Spirit of God allows us to call Him "Abba," which means "daddy."

As His adopted son, your Heavenly Father sees you as you were created to be - priceless.

Human beings are truly unique in all of creation both because we are made in God's image and because His children are the recipients of salvation through the Son.

The Great Lie

When your father failed you, you stopped believing that you had worth and value. You came to believe the lie that you had little or no value.

God's Truth

The truth is that the perfect Creator of the Universe says you have <u>infinite value</u> and that He loves you even as He loves His Son, Jesus.

Let's pause there for a moment.

Let that idea settle in. Breath in that truth deeply and invite it into every cell in your body, every memory and thought in your brain. Truly, at this very moment I urge you to embrace the truth of God's never-ending and limitless love for you. It is the catalyst of your healing. From that love and with your obedience you will learn to embrace, extend, and master forgiveness.

Applying the Truth, Daily

If you continue to see yourself through the lies of the past you will miss out on the wonderful benefits of being an adopted child of the King of the Universe. Living in the midst of the lies not only validates them as true in your life but it is calling God a liar. Because of your faith in Christ, God declares you perfect.

When you repent of your sins, you're forgiven. Period. Too often we allow the pain and sorrow and stress of life to dictate who we are, rather than believing who God says we are. The Apostle Peter tells us,

> *"His divine power has given us everything we need for a godly life through our knowledge of him who called us by his own glory and goodness. Through these he has given us his very great and precious promises, so that through them you may participate in the divine nature, having escaped the corruption in the world caused by evil desires."* 2 Peter 1:3-4 (NIV)

God gives us the power to live as His sons. It only requires that we submit to Him and obey His commands each day. When we daily apply the truths of Scripture to our lives, it changes us fundamentally from the inside out. Through that divine guidance and wisdom our hearts, minds, and behavior become aligned with the goal of becoming the man the Heavenly Father built us to be. In that transformation, we glorify Him.

Our Focus Matters

Choose to focus on the grace of God in your life, instead of your mistakes. The Lord has shown you the riches of His glory in Christ. The beauty of Christianity is that you are part of the body of Christ, His church, where you are knit together with other Christians so that we can build one another up and support each other. Together, we work towards the common goal to live and love like Jesus did.

You are not alone!

While your earthly father failed you, your Heavenly Father has not only healed you but given you a *true* family in the Church. We are all the adopted children of the King with the rights of royal children. We are no longer subject to this world but belong to the household of God.

Rejecting lifelong held lies takes disciplined practice and help from the Holy Spirit. Take time each day to ask God to forgive you for submitting to the lies that control your thoughts and actions. Here are a few examples:

- God, please forgive me for believing I am worthless. Help me to see myself as priceless and worthy of Christ's sacrifice.

- Lord, have mercy on me for hating my father for hurting me. Help me to forgive him as you have forgiven my sins in Christ.

- Father, today I feel like a total failure. Everything I touch fails. As your child, I know this is not who I am. Please help me to remember that I bring life to others because I have life in you.

By investing the time to evaluate your heart and actions during the day you can remind yourself of not only how God sees you, but of who you are in Christ. Your Christian brothers can also be a great source of encouragement if you will include them in your life and struggles. Be brave. Share with them where you are and invite their help. Allow the Light to shine upon the dark places. This allows them to rally around you and strengthen you. You'll be shocked at how ready some will be to share your burden and to battle in the trenches of soul warfare with you.

There is greater joy in the fight – and the victory – when you're in fellowship.

Knowing this truth is not enough, but truth must be put into action.

<u>Experiencing</u> the truth requires you to change how you live and think. The first step is making a conscious decision to open your heart to feel and know the forgiveness of God. Then you will be more willing to extend this forgiveness to others. If you believe in your heart and mind He has forgiven and adopted you, then you will imitate Him by forgiving your earthly father.

Two steps forward, one back, then three steps forward…

Don't be surprised if your spiritual progress (sanctification) is not a linear and totally positive progression from where your heart is now and where it will come to be - in total submission to the Lord and in forgiveness to others. Throughout this process it is natural to briefly slip back into negative self-talk, self-thought, and self-defense – even rebellion perhaps – as you take this fundamentally different path in your life. After all, you've had a lifetime of experience believing the lies. And let's face it. Satan himself loves and welcomes your retreat to a state of weakness, hopelessness, hate, bitterness, and victimization. Don't give him that power.

The second you feel your emotional focus and resolve to forgive slip, get on your knees and ask the Holy Spirit for help.

Experiencing true forgiveness will bring a powerful pivot in your focus, from dwelling on the hurt or the lies that came from the hurt, to feeling compassion for the one who hurt you. A contrite heart that humbly acknowledges one's own need for God's forgiveness will want the individual who harmed them to see their sin and repent SO they might find true, eternal life in Christ.

Authentic forgiveness is key.

| Chapter 5: Study |

As a reminder, this section is designed to help you work through the healing process. It requires an open and honest heart that desires to experience the healing of God. We encourage you to write down your answers in an electronic document or a journal so that you can refer back to them later as you begin to write your *Forgiveness Letter*.

NEXT STEPS: Working through the chapter

a. Answer the question, "Why did God allow this to happen?" Do you find comfort in your answer? Why or why not?

b. Compare the list of lies that you used to believe (from previous chapter) to these Scriptures about how God sees you.

c. Write a list of practical ways you can replace the former lies with the God's truth, daily.

d. Believing the many truths God declares about you requires you to learn to forgive others as He has forgiven you. It's not optional. Who must you forgive?

GET ROLLING with the <u>Companion Guide</u>: Preparation to write a *Forgiveness Letter*:

- Utilize the *Man Enough to Forgive* Personal Study Journal workbook

| Scripture References |

1. Don't think like children. Act like adults. 1 Corinthians 14:20 (NIV)

2. God's original creation was perfect, without suffering. Genesis 1 (NASB)

3. Adam's disobedience issued sin into the world. Genesis 3 (NASB)

4. With sin came corruption and suffering into the world. Romans 5:12-21; 2 Peter 2:19 (NASB)

5. The punishment for sin is death. Romans 3:23; 6:23 (NASB)

6. Like Christ, the world will hate us for righteousness. Matthew 10:22; John 15:18 (NASB)

7. God sent His only Son to die on the cross for our sins. 1 John 4:9-10 (NASB)

8. God sent the Holy Spirit to guide, guard, and as a guarantee of salvation. Matthew 13:1-11; Romans 5:3-5; Hebrews 10:12-23 (NASB)

9. All things work together for good, for those who are called to God's purpose. Romans 8:28-29 (NASB)

10. No one knows the Heavenly Father but his son, Jesus, and those He reveals the Father to. Matthew 11:27 (NASB)

11. Because of Christ, we can be adopted sons of the Heavenly Father. Galatians 4:4-5 (NASB)

12. We are redeemed from our sins by the blood of Jesus Christ. Ephesians 1:7 (NASB)

13. God sent the Spirit of His Son into our hearts to free us from our slavery to sin. Galatians 4:6-7 (NASB)

14. God's given us everything we need to live a godly life and escape evil desires. 2 Peter 1:3-4 (NIV)

headship

[head·ship] **noun**

Male headship will not be replaced. Truth does not disappear. God's foundational order is integral to nature, grace, creation, and salvation.

CHAPTER SIX

The Fatherless Man I Became

"and My anger will be kindled, and I will kill you with the sword, and your wives shall become widows and your children fatherless".
Exodus 22:24 (NASB)

| Quick Start |

Every man is led into manhood by someone. Our Heavenly Father designed that to be our biological father.

Sadly, because our world is warped by sin and corruption many men never had the honor of being led into maturity by their actual father. Too often young men's only example of manhood in their home was their mother's boyfriends. In that scenario boys witness firsthand what a lack of commitment does to family relationships and are sent the message "any man will due" as a stand-in father figure. Tragically, these temporary surrogates often manipulate boys and feed them harmful lies to get to their mothers.

Maybe your mother got married again and you had a stepfather - or two or three. Some stepfathers make an honest attempt at giving a boy *most* of what the biological father should have. But even having a good stepfather does not erase the pain of being left behind by your natural father. Others have great difficulty connecting with a stepson. In a mixed family environment, men often struggle treating their non-biological children with the same love and structure as their biological children.

Other times, even if the stepfather is well-intended, it is the mother who hampers the bonding process and interferes in the man's leadership role because of her own insecurities. Her false presumption is that being the boy's blood-relative preempts the man's role; *her* son is *her* responsibility. Perhaps you had male family members who stepped into the father void, or a compassionate neighbor who helped out periodically when his schedule permitted. There were likely some male mentors in your life, whether it be at church, sports, friend of the family, etc. but each of these lacked a clear commitment directed to you personally.

Despite having some good influences, you likely ended up struggling into manhood and continue to struggle now with the man you became before your faith in Christ Jesus.

You might have become a loner with few friends who struggles with commitment; may have become addicted to a myriad of ills, from pornography, to gluttony, to perfection, to gambling, to rage; became an abuser of drugs or alcohol, trying to drown the pain and hurt by numbing your entire body; went to prison because you allowed those around you to direct your path; became a workaholic whose drive to provide and achieve your own dreams became the most important thing and an idol in your life; in all these life choices you likely abandoned your own children to some degree because it was easier to follow your father's example and leave when it got tough.

My point here is that no matter the trouble, those life issues are all symptoms of the absence of a solid Christian father to shape and guide you in the home as you grew up, and all have their root in your father's betrayal to his biblical roles ordained by God.

No matter how you became the man you are today, God can and will continue to transform you into the image of Jesus. Some men have a particularly difficult time facing their own shortcomings and going through the process of forgiving their father and themselves because of deep and crippling guilt. Because they have, in one or more ways, followed in the footsteps of their father and failed or are failing today in their own role as fathers, they do not feel they are forgivable. This is understandable, because our behavior is our own choice, regardless of our upbringing.

If that is you, let me encourage you now.

Let today be the day you post your flag in the sand and say with conviction, "here begins the turnaround." Like the prodigal son, the Heavenly Father rejoices in the repentant son who returns to him for help, guidance, and protection. He will be with you as you seek to change your behavior and restore your position and relationship with your children. Unless they have passed away, there is time to reconnect with your children.

If you are truly repentant for abandoning them or failing in your role as Provider, Protector, and Pastor, then you will travel any distance and do all that is in your power to find them and make yourself heard. The Holy Spirit will give you the wisdom and strength to fulfill your job as a father and to make you into the man God intended you to be.
Learning to forgive your earthly father is a huge step in that process.

| Road Map |

The journey from boyhood to manhood is difficult even under the best of circumstances.

With your father absent and/or failing to honor God's command to lead you, the journey of going from an immature child to a healthy and well-adjusted Christ-following man became nearly impossible. Our society tells us that we don't need our fathers to teach us to be men, but that is a lie. A man is required to instill the vision and model biblical manhood. Your mother couldn't lead you in this way because she isn't a man.

In this chapter, we consider the men that led you into manhood and how that shaped the man you have become. The Christian man you are today is greatly influenced by your relationship with God in Christ, through the indwelling Holy Spirit and your relationships to other men in the church. In order to forgive your father, you must be able to understand and acknowledge the deficiencies and opportunities lost by his abandonment and the negative consequences resident in your life because of his lack of protection and pastoring.

WHO LEAD YOU INTO MANHOOD?

Mom's Boyfriend(s):

With your father gone it is likely that your mother dated, even if only sporadically, and her boyfriend(s) took on the role of leading you into manhood, whether they tried to or not. This man or men had no written or spoken commitment to your mother, as they were not married, and so his commitment to you was less than complete too. Maybe he tried to lead you but was always afraid of overstepping your mother's authority and such was only partially engaged. He could have been physically or verbally abusive, causing you further to question your worth and value.

Many of these men promise the children of single mothers the moon so they can "get in" with the woman, who quite naturally is looking to fill the void of male mentor in the home, but never intend to fulfill these promises. In all of these scenarios a boyfriend is a temporary leader that lacks both intentionality and commitment to leading a boy into manhood. The unstable and transient nature of these relationships prevented bonding, eroded the security of the son, and engendered cynicism in the youth about committed relationships and marriage.

In my personal experience and through helping fatherless boys for nearly two decades with Fathers in the Field ministry, fatherless boys feel/believe they got abandoned an average of 7 times by the time they are adults as a result of all the different men in and out of their lives.

Stepdad(s):

Your mom may have remarried, perhaps multiple times. Some stepfathers do step-up and intentionally lead their stepsons into manhood as if they were their biological children. It is possible your stepfather did an excellent job in this regard.

Unfortunately, though, many stepfathers struggle to lead their stepsons fully into manhood because of the unique relationship between a formerly single mother and her son. This can cause a boy to feel unwanted, worthless, or confused as to where his place in the family is. Statistically, second marriages with children present are more than 71% likely to end in divorce. As such, it is very possible you were abandoned by a stepfather too, creating a new, additional abandonment wound.

Neighbor(s):

For some boys it was a family friend or neighbor who recognized their plight and pitched in to help. This man witnessed the boy struggling to navigate life in ways a father would naturally guide and by volunteered to help, becoming a role model in one fashion or another. Deep down, you knew that while this man cared for and taught you some positive things, he had no intentional or lasting commitment to you. He was a temporary influence and a man to follow - but not one to *lead* you over time. Many other fatherless boys are not fortunate enough to have a good neighbor *or* family friend to help them and to follow after.

Because of the expense of raising a family alone on her sole salary or with marginal state assisted-income, boys in single-mother led families often they grow up in apartment complexes or in low income areas. Crime is more rampant in these parts of town for a variety of reasons, but here it can be criminal elements that become the most influential model for boys going into manhood. The criminal who appears strong and independent has money and its trappings. He may be willing to take a boy under his guidance. In him the boy sees a man not afraid of what he is and who treats him like a man, offering him a place to belong where he has value. The man only sees a boy who is expendable and can be used to his advantage.

Here again is a man for the boy to follow but not a true leader who will guide, correct, protect and teach a boy how to become a man of God.

Family:

Maybe you were blessed with an uncle, a grandfather, or other male family member to lead you into manhood.

The bond of family can be strong and long lasting, but still cannot replace the leadership of a father in the home. God commanded the men in Israel to care for the children and wife of their brothers, neighbors, etc. and to care for their property until the oldest boy could take over. They were told to lead these boys as they would their own sons. Generally speaking and unfortunately, American culture today has no such traditions. As a result, too often family will not step-in to help raise boys well or they live so far away that regular help is impossible.

Even when family members do attempt to help in the nurturing and guidance of a young man into manhood, the steps in their commitment often lacks intentionality, regularity and impartiality. A boy spending the summer on a family farm, far from his mother, for a period of time might receive a good dose of leadership, but that experience is offset or unwound by the other nine months at home. Provided he is a godly man and in sufficient health, (and interested in occupying this role), living with grandpa can help provide some biblical male leadership, but it usually falls short of the father-son dynamic.

You understand my point here; having an involved family is great and can provide some assistance in the youth guiding process, but it requires significant intentionality and additional commitment.

Mentor(s):

A mentor is an experienced or trusted advisor and guide. Most men have at least two men, in addition to their father, who they considered mentors as they grew from boyhood into manhood. Fatherless boys too can usually identify one or two mentors.

Others, sadly, had none. Who were your mentors growing up? Were they men who intentionally committed to helping you grow into the man God intended you to be? Maybe they attended your church, were a club leader, a teacher, coach, etc. They were able to teach you about life and how to get along in the world, but they lacked a formal commitment to you and often mentored several other boys at the same time. This caused you to compete or only hope for more of their attention which was a daunting task - especially if you *already* struggled with self-worth, confidence, and had a perverted sense of value.

THE TYPE OF MAN I BECAME:

Loner:

It became obvious to you early on that you could only trust yourself.

By not allowing others into your life, you believed you could keep yourself from being hurt. You isolated yourself as much as possible from other people. This perpetuated the belief that others will only fail you and that you are better off without them. Part of you longed for deep friendships but you struggled with investing in them because it opened you up to more disappointment. If you have children now, you struggle to have deep relationships with them as well.

As a man living a Christian life, you cannot remain a loner. Being secluded and isolated is like having a cancer that is slowly spreading through your body, killing you off a piece at a time. The Christian life is one of fellowship with others. We are built up, supported, inspired, engaged and held accountable by others, men especially, as "iron sharpens iron."

The Scripture tells us that,

> *"Therefore, if anyone is in Christ, he is a new creature; the old things passed away; behold, new things have come."*
> 2 Corinthians 5:17 (NASB)

The old you is gone and the new you is being made into the likeness of Jesus, filled with the Holy Spirit and is part of the body of Christ (1 Corinthians 12) so that the whole church might bring glory to God.

You cannot be an effective part of the Church (the body of Christ) as a loner. It takes time to learn to trust others. Christians will still fail you at times, but it is a vital part of becoming the man God designed you to be. This is not to say you need to become something you're not, or a totally different extroverted or gregarious personality. But you *do* need to be willing to share of yourself and be open to other Christians in order to be part of their lives.

Troubled Kid, Troubled Adult:

If you ended up in trouble with the law, or maybe even went to prison, the reasons may vary. Likely, a man or mentor-like male influence who led you into manhood was also a criminal, a gang member, drug dealer, etc. Or perhaps your own father was in jail and it seemed it was your destiny to end up there too. More than 85% of fatherless boys have some significant run-in with the law in their lifetime. This likely has a direct causal connection to who led them into manhood.

Being fatherless does not excuse personal responsibility for your incarceration; you did the crime and served your sentence. The time you spent in jail was undoubtedly difficult and traumatizing, often leaving scars that may never fully heal on this side of heaven. While this experience shaped the man you became thereafter, it is not the man God designed you to be big picture. He desires to *continue* to transform you, starting now.

Being a prisoner is not who you are, even if you are currently locked up. As a Christian you have been set free from the prison of sin and forsakenness.

> *"Jesus answered them, 'Truly, truly, I say to you, everyone who commits sin is a slave to sin. The slave does not remain in the house forever; the son remains forever. So if the Son sets you free, you will be free indeed.'"* John 8:34-36 (NASB)

You desire forgiveness and a fresh start for the crime you committed or hurt you caused, but you must first forgive those who harmed you, starting with your father. As you imitate God by forgiving others, it allows you to go to those *you* harmed with an open and contrite heart and ask them to grant the same forgiveness to you.

Addict:

Your father was gone. The brokenness became too much for you to bear and you sought to "escape" the pain through distractions that became addictions. Mind altering substances and behaviors of all types, whether it be sex or gambling, food, actual drugs and alcohol - or even work, when abused become drugs. You may have thought that drugs provided some temporary refuge. The people around you who seemed to be *like* a family were instead just a gateway to these drugs, and they added to the temptation to lose yourself in a "less painful" lifestyle.

While the drugs never permanently removed the pain, living in a semi-blissful haze made the days at least somewhat more tolerable. The days led to weeks, then months, then years and to an addiction that stopped covering your pain and only served as a source of it. The waves of helplessness, craving and shame still likely haunt you at times, even if you find yourself in a less acute stage addiction or (hopefully) free of it entirely.

Unhealed through forgiveness and your relationship with Christ, substance abuse and its accompanying triggers will follow you the rest of your life. With that said, there is true freedom from the desire for these pain maskers in our relationship with God through Jesus Christ. It will be particularly challenging to submit to God's commands, to really forgive and to accept forgiveness if you're actively battling addictions too. As stated above, God declares we are no longer slaves to sin, but being can be conformed to the image of Christ.

God *wants* us to be fully free to live in the flow of his love and mercy.

Workaholic:

You took a more "productive" approach to distracting yourself from your pain. You set your focus on goals and aspirational dreams and vowed that no one would hold you back. Rather than allowing the criminal elements around you or the guide-less home environment to influence you, you led *yourself* into manhood by redirecting your attention (and pain) with a laser-like focus. After all, maybe your dad would see all of your accomplishments, awards, and accolades and come back.

While you probably did some great things, later on as an adult the price paid for your obsessive, achievement-driven life approach was (or is) the relationship with your wife and children. You don't know how to be a good father, so you work long hours to put food on the table, clothes on their backs, and allow this "provision" to be the reason you are never there. If this didn't cause a divorce of your marriage yet, or estrangement with your children, it will.

Guess what? You can't do enough good things to impress God or to offset abandoning the roles as husband and father that He established for you.

You can't earn your way to heaven by means of meeting goals and your earthly achievements. The Lord insists that our relationship with Him be primary in our life. Second only to Him, our relationship and responsibility is with our family. And squarely behind family is *all* other relationships. By placing work as the highest focus in your life, you are worshiping it rather than God. Having your relationships out of sync causes only problems.

This may seem like an impossible value system to realign, but in truth it is easily fixed. Simply work less and make the love of God your primary goal. Will this have potential consequences to what you used to value most, to your income or professional recognition or to the ability to acquire more "stuff"? Sure. But when you do this you will begin to actually see the greater spiritual and relational needs of your family. You'll want to make the changes necessary and acknowledge that only *you* can be successful in this – your God-ordained job.

The burden to lead your family daily in prayer and reading Scripture will increase and as you fulfill the role of pastor. And trust me, brother, you will see your relationships deepen and the fruit of your changes in ways that will bring you far greater and lasting joy than anything you experienced before.

Absent Father:

With your own father missing or serving as a less than godly example of fatherhood, you found yourself imitating him and abandoning your own children. This breaks your heart now because the last thing you wanted was to abandon your own children and hurt them as you were hurt. Maybe you got your girlfriend pregnant and fought to make sure she didn't end the baby's life with abortion. You worked hard to be included in the life of your child and tried to stick around but it just seemed too hard.

Or, it could be that she made your life miserable, always nagging, fighting and pouring negativity into the family. You tried to make it work, but you had no solid example of how to do that, so you split.

Your intention was always to be there for your kids, but as the years went on you discovered you were just like your father. You didn't work hard enough to plead for what was best for your children. Failing to move heaven and earth to keep present in their life(s), you took the easy way out and left them behind to fend for themselves. No matter the scenario you left your children without their father to pastor, provide, and protect them. You failed and they are wounded just like you are.

SO WHAT NOW?

A Message of Hope for Generational Offenders of Abandonment

Especially for fathers who have repeated the sins and poor example of their dad and left the marriage and their sons behind, I'm asked, "John, what can I do now?" There is no one answer to this question, however, as the individual family situations dictate the access fathers have to their children.

That said, my first piece of advice applies to the dad who is separated from their son: you do *whatever* it takes to re-enter your son's life, beginning with seeking his forgiveness and you do *whatever* it takes to be there for him here forward.

I mean <u>everything and anything</u>. Move residences? Yes. Take another job that allows you to live close to him and spend time with him? Yes. I'm telling you – in virtually every discussion I have had with dads who are in this situation, all of the objections I hear come down to one thing: how badly he wants to make it right and to become the Christian father he's supposed to be.

But what about dads who are, legally or otherwise, legitimately prevented from having contact with his son? Here is something that *absolutely every dad can do*. I share this all the time with hurting fathers.

You can write your son a letter every day or every week that you are apart. You tell him about your life, how important he is to you, that you're thinking and praying for him. Be sure to date the letters and mail one copy to the home where he lives and keep a second copy. If the mail gets through, you will have accomplished the goal of at least letting your son know he is loved and you desire to be in his life to share the lessons you learn as you too develop spiritually. If the mail goes undelivered, or is not given to the child. Once your son turns 18 years old and is no longer restricted by the rules of his mother, (or legal restriction in some cases,) you give ALL those unreceived letters to him in a binder.

You prove to your son that he was constantly on your mind and in heart.

While you failed him deeply at some point that resulted in you being absent, you did what you could thereafter to pursue and restore a loving relationship with him. And then you earnestly pray, you have enduring patience, and if your son allows you to, continue to pursue him into adulthood. You'll always be his father, but perhaps you can once again become his dad.

There is always time to reconnect with your children unless they have died. If you are truly repentant for abandoning them, then you will travel any distance and do all that is in your power to find them and make yourself heard.

It requires you to go to them and apologize for leaving; to ask for them to begin the process of forgiving you. You cannot expect this forgiveness to come immediately but through the power of the Holy Spirit at work in your life you can help them begin.

A father's job of leading his children may shift over time, it only ends with death. Until then it is still your assigned job from God Almighty Himself.

Chapter 6: Study

NEXT STEPS: Working through the chapter

a. Did your dad marry your mom? Did he never commit to her (and you) or did they get a divorce – break their promise?

Fill in these statements for yourself:

b. My earthly father's example caused me to (*actions*) and I harbor unforgiveness towards him.

c. My mother's boyfriends or my stepfather affected me in these ways: (*impacts*).

d. If my father had been present these things would have been different: (*ways*).

e. Despite the mentoring of these men (*names here*) I still needed my father to be there for me, these reasons: (*reasons*).

GET ROLLING with the <u>Companion Guide</u>: Preparation to write a *Forgiveness Letter:*

- Utilize the *Man Enough to Forgive* Personal Study Journal workbook

Scripture References

1. You are a new creature in Christ. 2 Corinthians 5:17 (NASB)

2. You are a part of the body of Christ. 1 Corinthians 12 (NASB)

3. If Jesus sets you free from sin, you're free – period. John 8:34-36 (NASB)

The Walking Wounded

SERIES THREE

There is Healing

Step onto the Battlefield

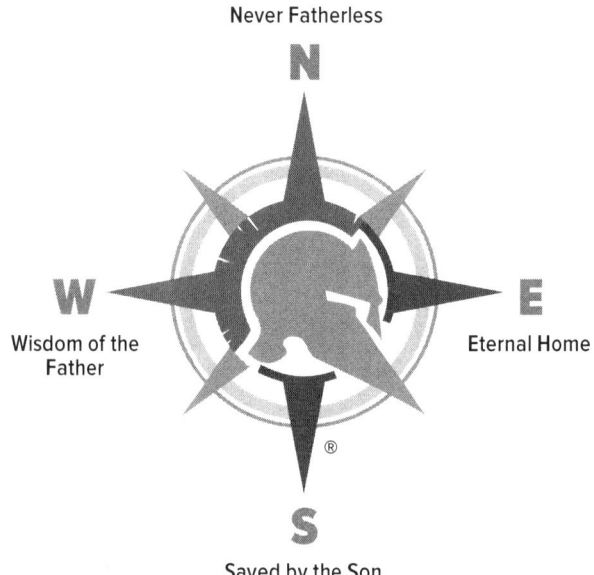

obedience

[obe·di·ence] **noun**

Carrying out the Word and Will of God. A positive, active response to knowing and experiencing God's blessings and favor. God's pleasure is not in sacrifice but in obedience.

CHAPTER SEVEN

Understanding Unforgiveness

"How blessed is he whose transgression is forgiven, whose sin is covered! How blessed is the man to whom the Lord does not impute iniquity, and in whose spirit, there is no deceit! When I kept silent about my sin, my body wasted away through my groaning all day long."
Psalm 32:1-3 (NASB)

| Quick Start |

In the Garden of Eden, Adam disobeyed the command of God to not eat from the Tree of the Knowledge of Good and Evil. When he did, sin entered the world, bringing death and corruption.

At its foundation, sin is disobedience of God commands, putting your own selfish desires at the core of your life. At the heart of unforgiveness is a selfish desire for vengeance or payback on your father in response to his sins towards you.

Unforgiveness either drives the desire for retribution against the person who has wronged you or develops a self-righteous attitude of this wrong doing as the unforgiveable sin.

Because your father abandoned you, you might wish him misfortune or even great harm so that he can understand the depth of your pain and heartache. Or even, Hell was specifically made for him. God requires believers to imitate the forgiveness they experience in Christ (Matthew 18:21-35).

This may sound harsh, but if you refuse to forgive your father it may actually be worse than his sin against you.

In order to truly experience life in Christ, you must move from unforgiveness to forgiveness.

Forgiving your father for maltreating and abandoning his fatherly roles is not pardoning or an endorsement of his sins. However, forgiveness does empower you, and it does make a strong statement saying, "I will not let the wrong you have done to me drive or dictate my decisions to live faithfully." It is evidence that you have experienced and understand the Lord's forgiveness towards you.

Your true and mindful realization of Jesus' forgiveness of your sins will give you the ability and the responsibility to forgive others' sins against you. Holding on to unforgiveness, just so that you feel justified for your actions, is unhealthy and inconsistent with the new creation you are in Christ.

It's simple – you'll forgive your father because your Heavenly Father has forgiven you.

| Road Map |

God created the world and placed His cherished people, the very pinnacle of His creation, in it. Genesis 1:26 (NASB) tells us that,

> "Then God said, 'Let us make man in our image, after our likeness. And let them have dominion over the fish of the sea and over the birds of the heavens and over the livestock and over all the earth and over every creeping thing that creeps on the earth.'"

We were created in the image of God, designed to be in relationship with our Heavenly Father. But shortly thereafter Adam messed up. Now we live in a broken world because of mans' sin. Beyond our creation, we have a purpose. Humans were created to bring God glory in all that we say and do, but our sin prevents us from glorifying and worshiping God has He deserves.

Adam disobeyed God's command and ate from of the Tree of the Knowledge of Good and Evil. This "original sin" issued in death and corruption. At its core, sin is the disobedience of our Heavenly Father's commands. Sin drives us away from the worship and glorification of God and towards selfishness and a desire to make ourselves God. Your father abandoned you to pursue his own sinful and selfish desires.

God calls men to lead and care for their children, but your father chose instead to abandon these responsibilities.

Through his sin, your father did not value you as he should, he did not rescue you, made excuses for his absence, betrayed his role to Spiritually lead the home, and he undermined all of the other ways God has commanded men to lead and provide for their children.

Because we live in a broken and fallen world, all of our relationships are not perfect, and we will most certainly experience pain and heartache. We will also contribute to the pain and anguish of others through our own selfishness. As Believers, we are to be continually working at being more like Jesus in our behaviors every day, so we can bring glory to God. To pursue that goal, we must engage in an honest evaluation our own sin of unforgiveness and the corruption of our heart.

THE SINS OF ABANDONMENT AND LACK OF COMMITMENT

God commands fathers to be the Pastor, Provider, and Protector of their families. When a father does not fulfill the biblical roles for his children, (he abandons them), this selfish action is sinful and a direct disobedience of God's command and ushers in generational consequences.

The world wants to sugarcoat abandonment of fatherly roles because it is so pervasive.

By nature, it is sinful. Today's culture elevates everyone's "rights" and freedoms, shuns responsibilities and commitment, and challenges the concept of God's ultimate authority. To not recognize the abandonment of fatherly duties is a serious sin. While it is common, it is not normal and it certainly isn't God's plan for men, for fathers, or for families.

God is not a Liar.

Your father's lack of commitment falls into this category of sin and resulted in you being emotionally and spiritually damaged. Instead of being sacrificially committed to raising you, he chose his own desires before the natural and covenant commitment to you. This resulted in you feeling angry, bitter, worthless, anxious, insecure, and emotionally disconnected from those around you.

His lack of commitment was sinful and wrong.

Both the sins of abandonment and of a lack of commitment to a spouse are forbidden in the covenant of marriage. That is why God hates divorce. (Malachi 2:16)

Your father's lack of commitment may have first manifest itself in a refusal to marry your mother. Then it continued as he left his commitment to you by the wayside. The message he sent to you both is, "Neither of you are worth my commitment, my investment, my intentional care, or my self-sacrifice." We live in a broken world because of sin. It is important to understand the truth about marriage and fundamentally why God hates divorce.

God designed marriage to unite a man and woman together physically, emotionally, and spiritually. In Genesis 2:24 (NASB) of the Bible, the Lord directs,

> "For this reason, a man shall leave his father and his mother, and be joined to his wife; and they shall become one flesh."

When both man and woman say "I do" and commit to one another, it is supposed to be forever because they are no longer two individuals but one person. Additionally, God's Word compares the oneness and unity of the relationship between a married man and woman to what a Christians' relationship is like with God (Ephesians 5:31-33). The Heavenly Father is the head and we, collectively, are the body – together as one. We cannot separate ourselves from the Christ and the Church and expect to live as God intended.

Malachi 2:16 (NASB) graphically reminds us,

> *"Neither can a man separate from his wife and expect life to continue unmolested."*

This scripture declares that divorce stems from hatred and results in violence; violence against the man and woman involved and, by extension, against their offspring because divorce kills the marriage and rips the two people apart. God hates divorce because it destroys what He created and blessed.

Thus, fatherhood role abandonment as a result of divorce is never without dire consequences. Never.

Some men and women offer excuses that are just that: *excuses* to cover up sin. You may have heard, "Your mother and I stopped loving each other, but not you." I am not suggesting that your parents stopped loving you, but the hard truth is that they loved themselves and their freedom *more* than you. Divorce is a violent action that harms the couple and their children. Platitudes and excuses can never make it right. Divorce is the *ultimate* abandonment.

Also, to be clear and to underscore a vital truth, consider this: the beginning of the divorce may have begun in the discernment dating process to select the future mother (or father) of their children and marriage partner. I.e., making excuses for bad behavior or character traits, a quick marriage, premarital sex, avoidance of issues or red flags, not seeking marriage counseling before marriage, being unequally yoked, thinking you will be able to change this person, etc.

Marriage and the selection of your children's future mother is "the" main issue/decision in your fatherhood role.

God is not a liar. There are always consequences when the marriage cup is broken.

This is why being abandoned by your father and experiencing his lack of commitment left an emotional vacuum in your life. As a result, you lost both a clear sense of your worth and were left directionless in many ways. As discussed in previous chapters, this led you to make life choices that often resulted in destructive paths, hurting yourself and others along the way.

It also placed the seed of unforgiveness in your heart.

The Hard Truth

If unforgiveness is in your heart, it will continue to negatively influence your life's path and be responsible for you leaving a massive wake of destruction all around you.

STRUGGLING TO FORGIVE

Tough stuff that'll take some manly courage to overcome.

As men, we are built for righteous war. It's in our nature.

It's the survival of the fittest instinct that's then turbocharged by the impact of culturally endorsed sin. This selfishness and unforgiveness is reinforced and incessantly propagandized from the second we're born with messaging that promotes "me first" and "have it my way" along with "an eye-for-an-eye" and "payback is a bear."

Especially for us men who exhibit both a strong sense of righteousness combined with a stiff shot of pride, when we are wronged our desire can become not only for justice, but for vengeance.

Justice alone would mean that the person who wronged us would receive retribution or punishment in equal measure to their wrongdoing. For example, if someone poked out our right eye, justice calls for the right eye of the offender.

Quite frankly, spiritual justice is God's job. Are you better equipped than Him to issue this fairly?

Vengeance then *also* seeks to teach a painful lesson - to issue a beatdown. It is man's overreaching that lacks spiritual wisdom, maturity, and grace. It presumes the dealer of vengeance is superior, without error, and flawless himself. The desire for vengeance requires payback for the wrongdoing with interest. Vengeance wants to take both their eyes and punch them in the nose for good measure. It wants to inflate the responsive action to really get the point across that we have been injured.

Hurt People, Hurt People

When the hurt is emotional and spiritual, as the father role abandonment wound is, our reaction is to hold a grudge and withhold forgiveness as further fuel for this grudge. By dwelling on the hurt, our desire for vengeance increases and the it becomes a more pronounced struggle for us to forgive.

The deeper the hurt, the larger the grudge and the higher the hurdle to forgiveness.

There is often an internal struggle that feels like if we forgive our father for abandoning us it condones his actions and it sends a message to the world that his actions didn't hurt us in profound ways. Even if we love Jesus, in this sensitive part of our life, we hold on to our pain and have no mercy, no Christ-like compassion, and a lack of humility that is appropriate of all sinners.

The last thing we want to see is this cowardly man receive a "get out of jail free card" or to walk away unscathed with a pardon for all of his selfishness and sinful actions. We struggle to forgive because we don't actually understand the concepts of biblical forgiveness and biblical pardoning.

And, we haven't come to grips with the three key truths I've been emphasizing in *Man Enough to Forgive* so far:

1) Unforgiveness is sin. On top of your abundant hurt, if you fall into the trap of sinful unforgiveness – even though it was born of your

father's sin – you've got a <u>massive spiritual problem</u> of your own that breaks fellowship with God or can be a mark of an unregenerate heart.

2) Sin <u>separates you</u> from God and from His forgiving grace. We simply cannot afford to deny ourselves the much-needed forgiveness that the Heavenly Father desperately wants to extend to His children.

3) We're actively <u>hurting ourselves</u> and many others whom we love! By embracing and holding on to unforgiveness, you continue to give the hurt power in your life. You extend a sort of slavery to your past and those negative emotions that are the source of behavior that makes you "less than" the man you were designed to be.

Let's Get This Straight.

First, forgiving your father for abandoning you and all the other hurt he *poured* into your life is not a pardon of his sins. It says, "I will not let the wrong you have done to me drive or dictate my decisions and I am not requiring restitution from you."

Second, forgiveness is first *poured out* on us as believers through the sacrifice of Jesus. We did *nothing* to earn or deserve that forgiveness, but it is gifted to us because of the extreme love of our Heavenly Father to His children. As a Believer, regardless of our natural and self-protective feelings, we forgive others <u>because God has forgiven us</u>.

I will address this topic more in the chapter that follows, but God requires you to forgive people in the same way He has forgiven you.

THE SIN OF UNFORGIVENESS

The Forgiving Heavyweight Champion: Jesus Christ

God expects His people to imitate Him in all things, even in forgiving those who have wronged us. In an incredible and powerful parable, Jesus sets the stage (and the bar) for who we are to forgive, how much to forgive, and how often we *must* forgive.

Because we are to be like Jesus… WHO = YOU

Because we are to be like Jesus… HOW MUCH = LIMITLESS

Because we are to be like Jesus… HOW OFTEN = ALWAYS

Jesus taught this lesson to his beloved, but stubbornly masculine apostle, Peter here in Matthew 18:21-35 (NASB):

"Then Peter came up and said to him, "Lord, how often will my brother sin against me, and I forgive him? As many as seven times?" Jesus said to him, "I do not say to you seven times, but seventy times seven. "Therefore, the kingdom of heaven may be compared to a king who wished to settle accounts with his servants. When he began to settle, one was brought to him who owed him ten thousand talents. And since he could not pay, his master ordered him to be sold, with his wife and children and all that he had, and payment to be made.

So the servant fell on his knees, imploring him, 'Have patience with me, and I will pay you everything.' And out of pity for him, the master of that servant released him and forgave him the debt. But when that same servant went out, he found one of his fellow servants who owed him a hundred denarii, and seizing him, he began to choke him, saying, ' Pay what you owe.' So, his fellow servant fell down and pleaded with him, 'Have patience with me, and I will pay you.' He refused and went and put him in prison until he should pay the debt. When his fellow servants saw what had taken place, they were greatly distressed, and they went and reported to their master all that had taken place.

Then his master summoned him and said to him, 'You wicked servant! I forgave you all that debt because you pleaded with me. And should not you have had mercy on your fellow servant, as I had mercy on you?' And in anger his master delivered him to the jailers, until he should pay all his debt.

So also, my heavenly Father will do to every one of you, if you do not forgive your brother from your heart."

Hard Core

We can be such blockheads sometimes, right Men?

When it comes to justice and vengeance, in service to our selfish desires and preconceptions we can look for loopholes and ways to blur the <u>totally clear</u> teaching in this parable. We somehow want an exception to this rule that allows us to embrace our carnal desire (or actions) for payback – all while still depending on God's mercy and forgiveness of us – even at the risk of our eternal souls. But it doesn't work like that.

Jesus is crystal clear that the point of the parable is that we need to forgive the <u>all</u> the countless hurts others have inflicted on us since God has forgiven <u>all</u> the countless hurts we have done to Him and others.

The sin of unforgiveness is *worse* than the sins of abandonment and lack of commitment because you received forgiveness and mercy from God but now refuse to return it. You welch on your side of the deal. To deny forgiveness shows a deep selfishness and immaturity and is an affront to the King of the Universe. A bad idea that breaks fellowship with Him. Or, It could point to an underlying heart transformation issue that you sincerely and prayerfully need to contemplate.

Be afraid - very afraid.

Sadly, for many men – even those who have turned the corner from being a walking wounded – simply locked their pain away and went on with life. Things may look "better" in their lives. But still, this unforgiveness becomes a 1000 lb. stone that sits on their soul.

Remember, the Lord is omniscient. That's all-seeing and all-knowing. Your good works will not earn your way to heaven or to joyful and eternal reunion with your Heavenly Father. You can season and cook up a piece of spoiled meat, covering up its rancid state enough to eat it, but you'll throw it up later. There's no tricking God.

As my Christian brother, I love you enough to give you the unvarnished, hard truth about this critical issue. It's *that* important!

*"So then, my beloved, just as you have always obeyed, not as in my presence only, but now much more in my absence, **work out your salvation** with fear and trembling;"* Philippians 2:12 (NASB)

By <u>acknowledging</u> that unforgiveness is a deep, selfish sin, you begin to move towards an active forgiveness of your father. This is a key step that is required before you can truly understand the truths forthcoming in Chapter 10 where you will begin to imitate our Heavenly Father by <u>actually</u>, without a doubt, forgiving your earthly father.

| Chapter 7: Study |

NEXT STEPS: Working through the chapter

a. Was your dad abandoning you a sin that is forgivable? Why or Why not?

b. Be truthful. I refuse to forgive my father for (<u>list reasons</u>).

c. Are you angry at your mom for you becoming fatherless?

GET ROLLING with the <u>Companion Guide</u>: Preparation to write a *Forgiveness Letter*:

- Utilize the *Man Enough to Forgive* Personal Study Journal workbook

| Scripture References |

1. We are to imitate the forgiveness extended to us by Christ. Matthew 18:21-35 (NASB)

2. We are made in God's image and given dominion over all the earth's creatures. Genesis 1:26 (NASB)

3. A man is to leave his parents and join a woman in marriage, becoming one. Genesis 2:24 (NASB)

4. The Lord compares a man and woman's unity to the relationship between God and the Church. Ephesians 5:31-33 (NASB)

5. Man is not meant to separate from his wife and expect a smooth life. Malachi 2:16 (NASB)

6. We must have a limitless tank to forgiveness. We can't expect to be forgiven if we do not forgive. Matthew 18:21-35 (NASB)

commitment

[com·mit·ment] **noun**

A decision about whom one serves – God or oneself. Steadfast, unmovable, and always abounding in the work of the Lord, even unto death.

CHAPTER EIGHT

My Fatherlessness Affects/Affected Everyone around Me

"Listen to the word of the Lord, O sons of Israel, For the Lord has a case against the inhabitants of the land, because there is no faithfulness or kindness Or, knowledge of God in the land".
Hosea 4:1 (NASB)

| Quick Start |

The Heavenly Father's design for a biblical family is perfectly balanced, comprised of a mother, a father, and their biological children.

By God's design, the family has everything it needs. Both the father and the mother fulfill their unique, gender-specific roles in order to shepherd their children and help them grow, mature, and develop into the people God created them to be - the perfect combination of nurturing and masculinity.

When sin and death entered the world, this intentional and polarized design became distorted. Even though we live in a broken world we still need to work in conjunction with God through the Spirit to honor and strive for the family's original design.

This is why God Himself champions the fatherless and widows and commands us to do the same.

He desires to repair what sin has broken to give all good gifts to the objects of His love.

A family breaks down and suffers because of the sins of its leaders, the parents, in ways we don't often think about. Consider these sobering facts, presented from research conducted by the Heritage Foundation.

> *"The collapse of marriages, along with a dramatic rise in births to single women, is the most important cause of childhood poverty. Nearly three out of four poor families with children in America are headed by single parents. When a child's father is married to his mother, however, the probability of the child's living in poverty drops by 82 percent."*

While living in poverty does not necessarily push people into a life of crime, drug use, etc. it is the single most influential contributing factor to these social ills.

We have little control over other people's behavior, including their sinful actions, but we *do* have control over how we behave and respond in hope and truth. The wounds you've accumulated because of your father's abandonment of his responsibility to you as well as his role in the family are a prime example of consequences that of sin that are beyond your control. This terrible wound can drive boys to destructive behavior such as doing drugs, committing crime, homelessness, to becoming an obsessive and performance-driven student or workaholic, and even to suicide. While your devastation potentially drove you in a negative direction, you chose how you responded and are responsible for those choices.

Your actions had an effect on all your relationships both before you put your faith in Christ for salvation and since. Coming to receive and "own" this truth now requires you to make some amends. Take the time to create a list the people in your life who you have wronged and make an effort to restore those relationships. Some of these relationships will be improved by your honest and humble apology, supported by the evidence of your change of heart that can be witnessed in how you live your life now. Other relationships will require time and the rebuilding of trust, as well as the healing blessing of the Lord.

Seeking forgiveness and grace does not excuse responsibility for your or the other individual's actions. It is not a magic pill that makes the hurt go away.

However, it *is* the important first step in acknowledging the wrong done, admitting responsibility, and recognizing the long-term effects of the sin on the other person. It is the proof that you're willing to work towards restoration of that broken relationship.

And, obviously, there are no guarantees.

This chapter seeks to help you identify the broken relationships in your life and gives you practical ways to start healing these relationships. Pray over the list of people you have hurt and then boldly contact each of them to begin the healing process towards hopeful restoration of the relationships damaged by your actions. Besides your relationship with the Lord, your most important earthly relationships are with your family members. Start there and work your way through others on the list.

Remember, forgiveness is powerful and freeing to both the forgiver and the forgiven. It takes courage on both sides of the relationship.

It takes grit and some spiritual maturity. It's not easy, but you are man *enough* for the challenge.

| Road Map |

The events and choices we make not only shape our lives but also impact the lives of those around us. Being afflicted with a devastating father abandonment wound clearly influenced your behavior choices. And your actions made you the man you are today. This is not an excuse for bad behavior or a way to exempt yourself from personal accountability. However, a real understanding and an association of cause-and-effect will to help you to untangle the Gordian knot that is in your life. In this chapter we will consider statistics related to fatherlessness in America. It is very likely that somewhere in that data you'll see parts of your story.

You'll be able to honestly evaluate how your fatherlessness and actions influenced your past and consider how your life choices, both your past and present, are affecting those around you now.

Results of Fatherlessness

Here me clearly. I love this country deeply. I believe it is truly a nation that is uniquely tapped by God to be the global shining city on the hill, formed on Judeo-Christian principles that are the very foundation of everything that is good about who we are and what we've accomplished together. I even dare say, I am a patriot.

But I am also terribly concerned about the spiritual warfare that threatens to decimate that foundation – at great risk is its very soul.

Since the 1950's there's been a huge, evident slide away from the Christian values upon which our forefathers constructed this Republic, causing everyone from psychologists, to pastors, to popes to preach, "as goes the family, so goes the nation." Well-known evangelist Greg Laurie adds,

> "The family can live without the nation, but the nation cannot live without the family."

The culture in America today seems absolutely committed to removing men from families, to feminizing men, to rewriting the expectations of biblical masculinity, and to forever deconstructing God's design for the family. Perhaps because it sheds a light on what government feels is a runaway train, information gathered by the U.S. Census Bureau and other collection agencies that *could* highlight the full-scale effects of fatherlessness has not been updated in decades.

Even some churches shy away from addressing the problems of fatherlessness because it is so rampant, and they sometimes lack the courage to hold men accountable in this way. They take a blind eye to this widespread epidemic by failing to acknowledge that *all* children who grow up without their biological father in the home are <u>also</u> fatherless. In so doing, they cave to the perspective that "any man will do" in the home.

Even if someone is there as a fatherly stand-in, this will fail to address the pain of father abandonment in children.

The reality is that the lack of a biological father in the home creates wounds that need to be addressed directly, with the healing help of the Holy Spirit. God is the perfect, Holy Creator.

Consider these impact points that are directly associated to the epidemic of fatherlessness:

THE TRUTH HURTS

On average:

- 85% of male <u>inmates</u> in both youth and adult correctional facilities grew up fatherless.

- 75% of all adolescents in <u>chemical abuse</u> centers come from fatherless homes; 10 x the national average.

- 85% of children with <u>behavior problems</u> come from fatherless homes; 20 x the national average.

- 71% of all <u>high school dropouts</u> come from fatherless homes; 9 x the national average.

- 90% of all <u>homeless and runaway children</u> are from fatherless homes; 32 x the national average.

- 63% of <u>youth suicides</u> are from fatherless homes; 5 x the national average.

- 80% of <u>rapists with anger problems</u> come from fatherless homes; 14 x the national average.

- 15% of fatherless men have <u>marriages that end in divorce</u> directly due to their singular focus on personal achievement or other distractions from their families.

Children in fatherless homes have:

4 x risk of being raised in <u>poverty</u>

6 x the rate of <u>neglect</u>

8 x the rate of <u>maltreatment</u>

10 x the rate of <u>physical abuse</u>

40 x more likely for a preschooler to be <u>sexually abused</u>

100 x higher risk of <u>fatal abuse</u>

I was a "statistic." Dealing with the effects of fatherlessness

Author Warren Farrell, shared in his book "The Boy Crisis: Why Our Boys Are Struggling and What We Can Do About It," has found that being "Dad deprived" is a leading factor in males' increased mental illness, addiction, and suicide. He links the mass shootings in 53 developed countries to boys and men who lacked a father figure, and he specifically mentioned six mass shootings that have occurred in the United States in the 21st century.

Identifying the effects that arise from being fatherless is useful, but it is not a crutch or excuse for your personal choices.

> "The person who sins will die. The son will not bear the punishment for the father's iniquity, nor will the father bear the punishment for the son's iniquity; the righteousness of the righteous will be upon himself, and the wickedness of the wicked will be upon himself."
> Ezekiel 18:20 (NASB)

Honesty with oneself is the foundation of healing and accurately evaluating the effects of your behavior on those around you. Offering excuses for our faults and blaming one's troubles on others is a function of arrogance, denial and unforgiveness. Those behaviors are symptoms of being sinful people in a broken world.

These tendencies are often magnified in fatherless children and are bad habits that were emerged from immaturity.

Unfortunately, without spiritual development and forgiveness, those habits generally follow into adulthood. A mother teaches the 'blame game' to her children when she expresses her own hurt and abandonment, created by the children's father leaving, and blames it solely on him. Then kids tend to follow suit, attributing their own poor choices or shortcomings on their father.

While your father is responsible for his actions, so too are you.

Our natural instinct is to inflate our self-image to both extremes, perceiving ourselves much better than others in some ways and much worse in others. It helps us navigate the world in a way that both protects us and attempts to provide us happiness. When confronted by truths that contradict this self-image, our brains are forced into a state that psychologists call *cognitive dissonance*. Your brain is trying to sustain and make sense of two conflicting ideas at the same time.

To resolve this conflict, you have a choice – to either admit and face the truth or to make excuses to yourself for the lies you choose to believe.

If you stood before a judge for an offense and were sentenced with a punishment, the penalty was earned because *you* broke the law, *not* because your father abandoned you. Your father's actions likely set you on a poor course, but ultimately you chose to break the law.

Now you have yet another choice. You can look at yourself and proclaim, "I am a criminal and that is all I will ever be; it is who I am." Or you can say, "In the past I disregarded the law, but it is *no longer* who I am. My Heavenly Father created me to be like His Son. He has given me what I need to begin that Journey. My family deserves the man God intended me to be and not the man I have been." I encourage you to choose the latter.

Recognizing the error of your ways *and* embracing the Lord's view of you so you can trust His forgiveness will help you overcome every negative hurdle, poor choices, and bad habit that may have put you into one of the categories identified in the statistics presented earlier. You can only impact what happens today and here forward. You have the ability to choose to live the truth or remain in the lie.

Moving forward with courageous action can be difficult, but it is completely possible if we see ourselves in light of who we are in Jesus Christ.

In 2 Corinthians 5:17-20 (NASB) Paul says,

> ***"Therefore if anyone is in Christ***, *he is a new creature; the old things passed away; behold, new things have come. Now all these things are from God, who reconciled us to Himself through Christ and gave us the ministry of reconciliation, namely, that God was in Christ reconciling the world to Himself, not counting their trespasses against them, and He has committed to us the word of reconciliation.*
>
> *Therefore, we are ambassadors for Christ, as though God were making an appeal through us;* ***we beg you on behalf of Christ, be reconciled to God.****"*

There is profound truth in Paul's encouragement. First, you are a new creation. The old sinful selfish you is crucified with Christ and the new you is directed to live like Christ. You are given the Holy Spirit to live in you and the body of Christ, the Church, to is there to teach, disciple, and encourage you to live like Christ.

Second, you are an ambassador for God, here on earth representing the Kingdom of Heaven and your Heavenly Father. Your old actions do not represent God. It is time to confront those actions truthfully and learn to move past them. Reach out to the support system at your church and ask them to help you, so that you can begin to be the man, the husband, the father and the Christian that God has designed you to be.

HOW MY FATHERLESS CONDITION AFFECTED MY RELATIONSHIPS

As the Holy Spirit works in our lives, we can look at the **Hard Truth** statistics and honestly assess which of them apply to us and to others in our circle. The Spirit will battle against the schemes of the devil that seek to keep you "stuck" in your weak position. Together you'll break down the barriers of blame, the protective walls of denial, and the chains of guilt. This inevitably leads us to considering how our actions have affected those in our lives.

The following section will help you to assess the impact of your choices and develop a plan to assists those you've hurt with healing.

Mom

Many fatherless boys have unhealthy relationships with their mothers, especially if she made her son a surrogate spouse or the standing "man of the house."

Single moms can give their boys too much information about their personal adult lives and struggles. While mom has no personal experience with the maturing process of growing from boy-to-man, she may attempt to "make" her son a man long before he's truly ready.

This is the blind leading the blind and can create a challenging co-dependent relationship. In this type of dysfunctional relationship, they protect each other from outside threats and feed one another's bad habits. It is hard for these boys to separate from their mothers and often they end up in an extreme relationship, either being wholly submissive to them or dominating them.

Many hide in superficial relationships not wanting to make a full, covenantal commitment through marriage, thereby avoiding any sort of public failure. Or, in fantasy land intimacy in the soul damaging addiction to pornography.

Sometimes a co-dependent son is even abusive and cruel to his mother in an attempt to cleave and create the necessary and healthy separation that is missing in their relationship.

A growing trend given the expanding brokenness in families is the son who does not leave the home given his lack of masculine confidence and work-ethic drive to create a life of independence, but is stunted in his emotional and mental backbone to leave the nest. Others are momma's boys unhealthily attached to their mother's needs and direction which creates huge problems for his wife in the marriage relationship.

I could easily fill this page with a multitude of mother-son relationship scenarios, but you are likely familiar with the prototypes and have seen them play out in other families.

Take some time now to evaluate your feelings and actions towards your mother. What is or was healthy? What was unhealthy?

How has your fatherlessness affected this important relationship? If there was dysfunction, what part was your mom's doing? What are you responsible for?

Siblings

If you share the same biological father, your siblings are your closest relatives. Even if you had different fathers you are linked to them in special ways. When you were younger, you and your siblings probably clung to one another for protection and reassurance. Come the teenage years, fatherless boys tend to break from relationships that are more related to childhood and less to manhood and their growing desire for independence. This separation can include the close relationships with siblings and may be exasperated by the boy's acute adolescent angst or particularly bad behavior such as drug use, criminal acts, or gang affiliation, etc. The chances are high that some of *your* teenage actions and behaviors created distance between you and your siblings.

Maybe, as the oldest, you have or had an unhealthy perspective that somehow you are ultimately responsible to take care of your younger siblings at the expense of your family. Or maybe your siblings were the ones who introduced you to compromising behaviors and situations. The point is that, as a function of your fatherlessness, as you grew up you were probably harmed by your siblings and you hurt them in some fashion as well.

It is important to take an honest account of how these relationships were affected by being fatherless, so you can take responsibility for your actions and seek forgiveness where necessary.

Extended Family

Watching you suffer and make bad choices left your extended family feeling helpless and unsure how to help. Perhaps family members stepped into your life in a consistent and helpful way; mentoring you, loving you, maybe even raising you. If you rebelled or went rogue, it is possible that your destructive lifestyle left them feeling helpless and hurt. They bailed you out of countless situations, let you live with them, paid your past-due bills, continued to take you to rehab, or a myriad of other tragic situations. Your response to them was one of anger or calloused indifference, as if helping you was their duty and not the act of sacrificial love that it really was. Or, you became a perpetual dependent of your mother, family members whereby, they pay your rent or other expenses as an adult.

Sometimes we forget that others in our family were both directly and indirectly hurt when our father abandoned us. And in addition to that shared pain, these grandparents, aunts and uncles, etc. *also* personally experienced some of our destructive behaviors.

What an opportunity this is to deepen your relationship now and heal together!

We need to be willing and ready to go back to them and restore those relationships. In addition to being the *right thing* to do and to being *conditional to your own forgiveness*, when you go back to family to seek and give forgiveness, it is a wonderful witness of your faith. In fact, this forgiveness process might be some family member's first encounter with the Gospel and example of God's forgiveness in Christ Jesus. How cool would that be?!

Take this opportunity to start mending these relationships. Remember, it is not always what you did, but what you did not do.

Friends

Have you ever stopped to think about all the friends that you lost over the years and why they are gone? How many people distanced themselves from you because "you changed" due to your destructive lifestyle? Later on, did you lose some "trouble brothers" when you changed your ways and stopped the mischief? How did these changes in peers, friends, and the others you chose to be around differ when you were younger versus when you first became a Believer? How about now?

Even though you have a new life in Christ today, are the old fatherless behavior patterns still active in your friendships? Do outbursts of anger or the feelings that they are trying to take advantage of you cause you to sever relationships or distance yourself from your friends?

Evaluate both your lost friendships and current ones. Who needs to receive apologies or forgiveness and which relationships deserve to be strengthened?

Coworkers/Employees

By now you surely realize that your fatherless wounds aren't simply in the past. They shaped your very being.

Even if they are less prominent in your adult life or you've become adaptive and successful, they are still part of who you are today. How have your coworkers suffered from your abandonment wounds? Are you prone to lashing out at them? Have you been overly critical or passive-aggressive? Are you chronically late, sick, or do you miss work assignments frequently? Take the time to evaluate this and ask the Holy Spirit to help you be honest.

Maybe you're the boss now and it's *your* employees that suffer. Do you have unreasonably high expectations or are obsessive or compulsive? Are you impatient and short-tempered? Do you have trust issues and are worried that staff will bail on their responsibilities (and on you)? Do you find yourself frustrated that your employees can't meet the goals that you so easily reach? Many fatherless business leaders are so focused on achieving their personal goals and dreams that even their employees suffer and get caught in the process of making their business dreams a reality.

Given that fatherlessness is so common and rampant in our culture, you might even recognize the negative symptoms of the pain you suffer *in* your staff. The odds would indicate that 50% of your coworker men *also* bear the marks of father abandonment wounds.

Take some time to look at how you treat your employees, how you interact with them, etc.

Authority Figures

It is probably not possible for you to go back and seek forgiveness from all the authority figures in your past. Where it is possible, you should. This is a great chance to humble yourself, apologize and ask for their forgiveness for your maltreatment of them. In this way you show the changes God has brought and is bringing to your life. Again, what a witness you can be!

You might be surprised by how many apologize back to you or share their story of being healed through Christ.

How do you respond to those in authority over you now? For example, how do you react when a boss is constantly after you to improve your work and seems to make impossible demands? Do you find yourself being passive-aggressive or even outright confrontational? Maybe the stress created by those in authority have led you to self-medicate or to miss stretches of work. In an inappropriate fashion, perhaps you've put bosses and authority figures in the shoes/role of father figure.

Or maybe you've responded to their critique through the lens of criticism and rejection of your father and not plainly as just instructions; or, correction made in love.

Evaluate how you view and respond to authority and be honest with yourself about the struggles.

Your Wife

The fallacy of the "strong man."

Generally speaking, men hate to appear weak.

And, many men are not particularly strong at verbally communicating about their feelings. Add these two conditions and you have a *stoic man* who may find having open conversations about their fatherhood wound, about shame over their behavior, and about asking for forgiveness from their wife particularly difficult. But here's why you should do all three.

Women want men to be strong – yes. But they also crave intimacy, a man who can express a generosity of spirit and trust to share what's difficult for them to articulate. They want to be let-in and to connect with a man who is courageous enough to be vulnerable about the pain they've carried through life. You may find that this process of forgiveness serves as a platform for you to become even closer, more united as a couple, and to share a deeper level of spiritual intimacy with your wife.

As you learn about the nature and consequences of your fatherless wounds, bring your wife along for the journey.

Chances are, your wiliness to do so will surprise and delight her. She'll likely see your strength – not weakness – shine through. You can anticipate that as her understanding grows about your heart wounds and the life implications that followed, so too will her compassion for your struggles. You'll be leading her as a man should in spiritual development as well, being brave and committed to God's commands and drawn to His standards above your own. Allow her to be your partner in the process and trust her to offer feedback and some accountability as you heal. Next to the Lord and the Holy Spirit, your spouse should be your #1 support – but you must allow her to operate, learn, and grow in the role – without the fear that she too will just let you down.

Your wife made a vow to be with you until death, through all the good and bad circumstances of life. How have you treated her? Does she receive the love and leadership that she deserves as your wife? Too often, wives are the recipients of the frustration and anger husbands harbor towards others but do not dish out to them personally. Trust me, your wife is well aware of the variety of effects of your father abandonment wounds. She's been there to see how that manifests in your behavior throughout different experiences.

Evaluate how you speak to and treat your spouse. Are you taking the time to pray with her every day? Are you being the spiritual leader of your home by attending church regularly and leading a bible study with your wife and children? Or, are they only getting the obsessive, self-driven, self-centered you?

You made a commitment to your wife. This relationship needs to be the first to get healed and healthy.

Children/Grandchildren

Men are all about competency and they fear failure. We want to feel like we know what we are doing and that we won't fail in obvious ways. Being a fatherless man who is raising a child yourself, you had little or no good example of how to be a father. Instinctually you feel certain that you will (or have already) failed your children. This is why so many fatherless men abandon their children and end up passing along all the same wounds they suffered to their children. It is even possible that you have alienated your children and that they won't speak with you.

It is never too late to go to your children or grandchildren and ask them to forgive you. It may take time and require that the Holy Spirit change you profoundly – but it is worth it. Evaluate how you have harmed your children and possibly your grandchildren and ask God to show you what needs to take place to begin the healing. Humbling yourself in this way is also the best witness of how Jesus has changed you. As your offspring experience the new creation you are in Christ, they see a living testimony of the Gospel.

Sharing the Gospel and demonstrating God's grace in you is the greatest gift you can give them.

REPAIRING BROKEN RELATIONSHIPS

The brokenness you felt because of your abandonment wounds led to toxic choices and damaged relationships. The wake of destruction in your life might be minimal or it might have washed through like a massive tsunami, wiping out everything in its path. Either way, the relationships that were damaged need to be addressed and forgiveness sought in order for you to begin the healing process.

I asked you to evaluate your key relationships in the context of the categories discussed previously so you could be honest with yourself about who was hurt and how. Now I want to help you to be proactive in addressing these relationships in ways that honor God.

1. The first step is to make a list of the people you hurt and the specific ways you hurt each person. Write down the behaviors and situations you need to request forgiveness for, as well as the reasons they may need to be forgiven.

2. Ask God to help you to truly love the people on your list enough to go to them to restore your broken and damaged relationships. As I've noted before, you'll be aided and strengthened by the Holy Spirit, so don't fall victim to skipping this vital step or only going half-way in order to protect yourself from pain and embarrassment.

    It is hard to admit to others that our poor choices and selfishness damaged them, but we must in order to overcome our sinful past.

3. If possible, go and see each of these individuals in person or call them if you cannot travel to see them. Ask them to listen openly as you share your heart, even before they respond. If they say "no," then proceed the best you can. Tell them how you have been forgiven by Jesus Christ and that too you are trying to obey His command to seek the forgiveness of everyone you have wronged. And where appropriate, share that you're also committed to forgiving those who have hurt you.

Understand that some people will be quick to forgive, but most *will* also want to see your words reflected and supported by your actions.

4. Live your life in imitation of Christ. When you fail, own your mistakes and seek reconciliation. This takes the power of the Holy Spirit and daily submission to God in all things. Remember you are not that fatherless boy anymore. You're *man enough to forgive* and on the road to becoming the man God intended you to be.

5. When you fall short and fail, as we all do from time-to-time, try-and-try-again with resolve to improve how you seek forgiveness and forgive others. With the Lord, forgiveness isn't a one-shot deal. Neither should be your efforts as you work towards forgiving and making amends. Seeking perfection in oneself and others is a fool's errand. You've got a lifetime of experience, maybe a heartful of hurt, and probably some bad habits to overcome. It'll take some time and effort.

As you keep at it, especially when it's awkward or fatiguing, don't forget – it's so worth it!

The Abundant Blessings of Forgiveness

- A fully restored relationship with Jesus Christ.
- Your prayers can be heard (unconfessed sins thwarts prayer).
- You can love your spouse like Christ loves the Church.
- You can speak life, love, and biblical relationship wisdom into your children.
- You can serve the kingdom with a refreshed spirit.
- You can find joy in life no matter the circumstances.
- We are adopted into God's family.
- You can serve the kingdom by coming alongside and being an example to other men who are the walking wounded (like you used to be).
- You can be God's mighty warrior with being weighed down by the shame of the past.

Becoming the Man God Wanted You to Be

Forgiveness is the lynchpin to your relationship with the Heavenly Father. Similarly, forgiving and asking for forgiveness is a core spiritual skill that unlocks many of the maturity and growth characteristics that are part of becoming the man God wants you to be.

- **Self-Assurance and Confidence**

    "But you are a chosen people, a royal priesthood, a holy nation, a people for God's own possession, so that you may proclaim the excellencies of Him who has called you out of darkness into His marvelous light;" 1 Peter 2:9 (NASB)

- **Closeness with God**

    "Come close to God and He will come close to you. Cleanse your hands, you sinners; and purify your hearts, you double-minded." James 4:8 (NASB)

- **Personal Growth**

    "For I am confident of this very thing, that He who began a good work among you will complete it by the day of Christ Jesus." Philippians 1:6 (NASB)

- **Courage**

    "Have I not commanded you? Be strong and courageous! Do not be terrified nor dismayed, for the Lord your God is with you wherever you go." Joshua 1:9 (NASB)

- **Men in the Family Structure**

    "But as for you, proclaim the things which are fitting for sound doctrine. Older men are to be temperate, dignified, self-controlled, sound in faith, in love, in perseverance." Titus 2:1-2 (NASB)

- **A Better Father**

    "The father of the righteous will greatly rejoice, And he who fathers a wise son will be glad in him." Proverbs 23:24 (NASB)

- **A Better Husband**

"You husbands in the same way, live with your wives in an understanding way, as with someone weaker, since she is a woman; and show her honor as a fellow heir of the grace of life, so that your prayers will not be hindered."
1 Peter 3:7 (NASB)

- **A Better Friend**

"A friend loves at all times, And, a brother is born for adversity."
Proverbs 17:17 (NASB)

- **A Better Co-Worker and Leader**

"Whatever you do, do your work heartily, as for the Lord and not for people,"
Colossians 3:23 (NASB)

- **A Better Member of Church Family**

"Be on guard for yourselves and for all the flock, among which the Holy Spirit has made you overseers, to shepherd the church of God which He purchased with His own blood." Acts 20:28 (NASB)

- **Establish a Godly Legacy for Your Family**

"Be careful and listen to all these words which I am commanding you, so that it may go well for you and your sons after you forever, for you will be doing what is good and right in the sight of the Lord your God."
Deuteronomy 12:28 (NASB)

| Chapter 8: Study |

NEXT STEPS: Working through the chapter

a. I never stopped looking through the lenses of the child I was when dad left/died and my response was to treat mother and siblings like (*describe*).

b. I tried to fix my abandonment wound by doing (*list actions*) and instead of fixing it caused (*list consequences*).

c. The consequences of my not dealing with my fatherlessness cost me relationships and jobs because I continually did and said things like (*examples*).

d. Would/can you admit that you are a sinner? Why or why not?

e. My hurt turned into poor choices and toxic relationships. I need to make amends with these people (*list people*) for these hurts I inflicted.

f. I need to correct these sins (*list behaviors*) now to move forward.

GET ROLLING with the <u>Companion Guide</u>: Preparation to write a *Forgiveness Letter*:

- Utilize the *Man Enough to Forgive* Personal Study Journal workbook

| Scripture References |

1. Sin leads to death. Your sins are your own. Ezekiel 18:20 (NASB)

2. We are a new creation in Christ. Be reconciled with God! 2 Corinthians 5:17-20 (NASB)

3. Spiritual growth for men: Self-assurance and confidence. 1 Peter 2:9 (NASB)

4. Spiritual growth for men: Closeness with God. James 4:8 (NASB)

5. Spiritual growth for men: Personal Growth. Philippians 1:6 (NASB)

6. Spiritual growth for men: Courage. Joshua 1:9 (NASB)

7. Spiritual growth for men: Men in the Family. Titus 2:1-2 (NASB)

8. Spiritual growth for men: Being a great father. Proverbs 23:24 (NASB)

9. Spiritual growth for men: Being an excellent husband. 1 Peter 3:7 (NASB)

10. Spiritual growth for men: Being a good friend. Proverbs 17:17 (NASB)

11. Spiritual growth for men: Being a better co-worker and leader. Colossians 3:23 (NASB)

12. Spiritual growth for men: Being a better member of the Church. Acts 20:28 (NASB)

13. Spiritual growth for men: Establishing a godly family legacy. Deuteronomy 12:28 (NASB)

perseverance

[per·se·ver·ance] **noun**

Steadfastness in knowing God's plan is good towards His people, preserving to the end in and through God's sovereign plans that refine self and bring glory to God.

CHAPTER NINE

Dealing with the Emotional Hurts

"But if we are afflicted, it is for your comfort and salvation; or if we are comforted, it is for your comfort, which is effective in the patient enduring of the same sufferings which we also suffer;"
2 Corinthians 1:6 (NASB)

| **Quick Start** |

Dealing with pain and disappointment of your father wound can be difficult because it takes very little to evoke our habitual emotional responses.

You might see or hear something that reminds you of your dad or his absence and it releases an emotional roller-coaster. For some, these emotions may even be the cause of biophysical responses that you can't control. Of course, *we* can control our behaviors. The sooner you come to terms with your emotional hurts and begin to heal them, the sooner you can manage your responses to the situations in life that will occur.

You are not your emotions or feelings. You are what God Almighty says you are; a redeemed and adopted son of the Heavenly Father.

Some emotions elicit secondary responses such as anger, hysterics, crying, feeling worthless, etc. These responses are either an expression of the emotional wound or are masking or distracting responses in an attempt to protect you from experiencing further trauma. Identifying the underlying wound as well as any secondary response will allow you to develop intentional strategies to re-program negative associations and take a more proactive approach to behavior modification. Both are part of your healing process.

Other emotions fuel what are considered primary responses, like hatred. At the core of hatred is selfishness and unforgiveness. No wonder we so often hear fatherless boys (and men) say, "I hate my dad for leaving me." What can be challenging for fatherless men to accept is that *similar sin* is responsible for both the behaviors of abandoning one's family <u>and</u> choosing to hate someone else by refusing to forgive them. In fact, they're two sides of the same coin.

Another primary response that's related to the wound of father abandonment and betrayal is perfectionism. This one is tricky because pursuing excellence in all things for Christ is certainly worthy and biblical. In some cases, men may even use perfection as a standard by which to isolate and protect themselves from the sinful actions of others. However, when wrongly motivated and indulged perfectionism can also be the sinful elevation of oneself and the demeaning of others.

Dwelling on all of these emotional hurts and responses is ultimately a focus on yourself, rather than you being focused on the Lord and who He has made you to be, in Christ. When you placed your faith in Jesus for salvation, you became a new creature who is filled with the Holy Spirit. God has called you to imitate Christ and love what He loves, so you can no longer allow your primary focus to be on yourself, on how you were wronged, and on your pain.

Understanding this fundamental change of focus should motivate and encourage you to, once and for all, sort through the emotional baggage.

Fortunately, the healing power of the Holy Spirit will assist you in shifting your attention from your feelings and accounting for your wounds to what you should do *next*. Where you may have labored alone with this pain for years, He will help you break the silence of lonely suffering.

Road Map

The emotional damage of being fatherless is vast. Human beings were designed by God to have a wide range of emotions, and to learn to express and control them through the guidance of our parents for God's glory. When a father is absent from a boy's life, he will struggle not only with his self-worth but with how to express and control his emotions.

This chapter is designed to help you sort through some of these emotions. While many things in your life will naturally change as you get older, without additional perspective, guidance, and new motivations, emotions tend not to. They're primal.

As children, we were equipped with strong feelings of anger, resentment, fear, longing, sadness, and grief – even if we were not mature enough to understand and articulate them.

ANGER AND EMOTIONAL OUTBURSTS

Anger is almost always a secondary emotion, meaning that it is a *response* to a hurt that threatens the core of who we are as human beings. Angry outbursts do not always include violence, but often there is violence associated with the outburst. Anger alone is not the problem. It is a reflection of a deep hurt that is in need of healing.

This does not excuse the actions that erupt from an emotional state of anger, but it helps us to examine why we got angry in hopes of absolving the core hurt.

You may have been prone not only to outbursts of anger, but all types of strong emotional expressions such as crying, sadness, mania, or hysterics. Each of these outbursts has at their core a deep wound. These core hurts include, but are not limited to, feeling unimportant, unloved, worthless, powerless, and fearful. Anger and depression particularly can be self-protective emotions.

Sometimes we'll embrace the emotional state intentionally, because even though it's negative, it is familiar and predictable. It may even bring people's attention and focus on you that we may crave. In other cases, anger and depression is an unconscious state that is difficult to escape as a reaction because you were not taught proper ways to express and deal with your wounds or your emotions.

An important first step to healing from anger issues and controlling emotional outbursts is to first acknowledge that they are a response to a deeper emotional trauma. Second, you need to identify what type of emotional hurt it is being covered.

For example, you might come to conclusions like, "My dad left me, and I felt worthless. Whenever something or someone makes me feel worthless, I react with anger, or I cry, or I withdraw, etc. This is a defense mechanism to protect me from the emotional pain of being abandoned and from feeling weak and helpless."

Third, you'll begin the process of healing your trauma when you are able to understand the source of your pain and work at removing the lie at its core. Again, truth and light is the enemy of the evil one.

Remember, your Heavenly Father loves you and sees you as a most precious and valuable part of creation. His love for you is infinite and He has given you the Holy Spirit and the Church to support you through the healing process. As a fatherless man, asking other men to walk with you on this journey is difficult because you are openly admitting needs and weakness when your experience says men will fail you.

Your earthly father let you down, but you need to allow other Christian men to help you learn to heal and become the man God designed you to be.

THE PAIN OF LONELINESS

With broken promises often comes dashed expectations. This can lead to not only a sense of worthlessness, but to a deep sense of loneliness. As a boy, every day that your dad was gone your heart longed for him to be in your life in a relevant and powerful way. Into adulthood, while your need for provision and protection changed, you still feel the void of that missing role and relationship. This too brings loneliness. It may seem as if the pain of loneliness is the most powerful emotion in your life because it's the one that's always there – both on the emotional surface and beneath it. Even your anger is a tide that rises and falls more acutely, the pain of loneliness never leaves. And there's something unique about the loneliness that is associated with your father's abandonment.

You can have a life *full* of people – friends, a spouse and kids, co-workers, and many others – and yet *still* have a hole in your heart the shape of your missing father that is responsible for loneliness.

So how do you learn to heal from the feeling that you are alone in the world; that no one truly understands your pain; and that nothing seems to be truly getting better?

As a Christian, first you should remember that **your Heavenly Father is always with you and sees your infinite value and worth**. In the Bible, anytime a concept or principle is repeated, it's done to emphasize how important and fundamental our understanding of it is. Repetition is used for particularly difficult mandates, to make sure we know what is expected of us – even if it's tough. And repetition is used to clarify complex ideas.

In *Man Enough to Forgive*, you've probably recognized that I keep going back to a few fundamental statements and principles. Probably the greatest example of this is the truth about how much you are unconditionally loved and treasured by the Heavenly Father. I do this intentionally because this is a stark contrast to your earthly father, and it can be difficult to receive for the man who has fatherless wounds.

Secondly, make a concerted effort to meet other people and form deep friendships in Christ. Churches are a great place to meet people that typically share your values and spiritual worldview. This common bond helps to forge powerful friendships. Additionally, it is in the Church, the body of Christ, that we are supposed to learn about God and begin the process of healing our wounds.

Third, start to volunteer and give of yourself to other people. Christian leaders and even secular psychologists have long advocated that the fastest way to get over pain and depression is to serve others. Take the focus off yourself. Don't give your emotions and present attention to the ghosts of your past. Part of a relationship with God is for Believers to serve with Him in ministering to those who suffer from the results of sin and corruption – even if you too are still in that camp.

Sadly, your situation of being a man who is still harboring the pain of father abandonment is not unique. Isolation, pride, and shame make us feel alone, even when we aren't. You may have heard the adage, "When you give, you receive." It's true!

Additionally, when serving, you can meet other people who are currently or have gone through what you have. You can help each other see how God wants to heal you both. Loneliness is a part of having been abandoned, but it does not have to be the state in which you remain. It will consume you if you let it.

With God, we are never truly alone.

DEEP-SEATED HATRED OF YOUR FATHER OR YOURSELF

Unlike anger which is a secondary emotion that requires an object to receive the emotion, hate is a primary emotion and requires no object. Think of hate as the Swiss Army knife of the emotional realm, with love being its antithesis. In the same way you use a serrated blade for one purpose and a straight blade for another, so too can hatred perform specific destructive emotional tasks - slicing, ripping, and tearing at hearts when coupled with other emotional states.

When hatred is deeply rooted in your life it will act to effectively sever relationships and focus your energy into selfish pursuits to your ultimate destruction.

God IS love. Hatred is the active shunning of the Lord's very nature.

Where biblical love calls for you to place the needs of others above your own selfish wants and desires, hatred promotes the opposite. Hatred focuses your energy and emotions on destroying relationships and driving you towards fulfilling your deepest personal gratifications. Hatred kills healthy relationships, cuts out and discards those who love us, and encourages us to pursue outcomes that can destroy everything positive in our lives. As followers of Christ in both our words *and* deeds, there is no room for hatred in our lives.

If we've harbored hate, perhaps even feed and nurtured it with righteous indignation, we must now confront that sin. We need to seek the Lord's forgiveness and *work through* the realities from which that hate developed so we might imitate Christ in all aspects of our lives.

Take an honest and detailed look at your life right now and ask, "Where and how does hate play a role in my life? Do I hate my father? Do I hate myself? Is hatred a factor in how I live my life and relate to others?" If you answered "yes," to one or more of these questions, then one of the hardest parts – denial - is behind you. The truth is that most of us *do* hate or have hated before we made a conscious decision and commitment not to hate. Much like admitting that you have become addicted to any substance or harmful and repetitive behavior, admitting that you have allowed hatred to root in your life is challenging.

Temporarily, it could potentially erode some of the self confidence that you've worked so hard to develop – but it doesn't need to. In fact, if you MAN UP here to overcome hate, that can be a positive and deserving source of greater, Christian-centric self-worth in Christ.

So how do you begin to heal from the *damage* of your hatred?

Start by seeing hatred for what it is. Jesus tells us that hating a brother is as bad as murdering him (Matthew 5:21-22). Allowing your hatred to drive your thoughts and actions is akin to murdering the object of your hatred.

Let that sink in. Do you really want your father *dead*? If he was dead, your relationship could never be mended, and your father would have potentially passed on without reconciling with God.

Remember, there is an important distinction between reconciliation and forgiveness.

Do *you* really wish to be dead yourself (self-hatred)? Are you OK with having a "dead" spiritual life? Hatred leads only to death and separation from the love of God. In the Bible, the Apostle John puts it this way,

> *"Everyone who hates his brother is a murderer, and you know that no murderer has eternal life abiding in him. By this we know love, that he laid down his life for us, and we ought to lay down our lives for the brothers."* 1 John 3:15-16 (ESV).

Hatred is death.

As you forgive and heal from your fatherless wound, you will experience the love of God in Christ in a whole new way. When you respect the Lord's tenants, His rules, and His promises, your hate will be replaced with love and compassion.

The world is telling us to hate things that the Lord forgives. The world wants us to love things God hates - like broken families, greed and lust, tolerance for sin, moral relativism, abortion, demeaning of masculinity, and the list goes on and on.

Disagreement is *not* hate – even if it is sold that way by the media and liberal culture in America. Stand up for families? Stand up for the biblical definition of marriage as between one man and one woman? Stand up for the sanctity of human life? Stand up for the differences between men and women? Stand up for conservative Christian values in your home, church, and community?

If you're a true Believer who is living up to the biblical Christian standard, there's a good chance that you'll be labeled a "hater."

But you'll know this is simply another lie of the enemy.

Where do we learn to hate? Sadly, most young people learn to hate in the home, from their parents' examples of how they behave with one another and with their children. Maybe you have had a suicide in your family and learned self-hate. Then the culture steps in with its influence: media pundits, television, movies, the internet – and even in government schools and apostate churches. As boys are abandoned by their fathers, these lessons of vindictive conviction are easily applied and hate for the dad grows. Other boys simply become indifferent to dad, masking the pain and shutting him out, which is another expression of hate.

The Lord tells us to hate only one thing – sin. So now, with this frame of reference, we cannot embrace hate for one second longer or perpetuate a "he deserves it" narrative that excuses ourselves for the sin of hate. In fact, the sins that were done to you have consequently led you directly down the path of sin as well.

You can and must stop the cycle.

Frankly, as they get older, most men are willing to "move on" from the pain and wounds of their father's abandonment, but they are *very* reluctant to release their hate because they think it endorses or excuses the hurtful behavior. It doesn't. But you cannot both forgive and still hate your dad. Letting go of one's hate does not excuse the wrongdoing of others. It is a recognition of a greater need - the need to be forgiven themselves. Your father needs to experience the love and forgiveness of Christ just like you did.

Let your hate die an appropriate death, sending it right back to its maker – Satan.

You have the indwelling Holy Spirit who will equip you with the ability to forgive and allow hatred to be ripped from your heart and replaced with a love that mirrors God's Love. It is not enough to simply acknowledge that you struggle with hatred. You need give your hate over to God, asking that He heal you so that you can be a solid witness for Christ to those you once hated.

Will you be *man enough* to ask God to do this?

ABIDING FEAR

As strong an emotion as hate is, fear may be even stronger.

When a negative emotion, fear is even more tricky because whereas hate is universally bad unless it is a healthy disgust for unbiblical truths and sin. Fear can be wildly destructive but also *some* fear can be appropriate. Righteous fear of the Lord represents our respect, our deep reverence for Him. As long as it is controlled, moderate situational fear can sharpen awareness, can be motivational, and can clarify.

Abiding fear, however, is generally crippling. Abiding fears are those that remain with you even after you feel like you have healed from the trauma of abandonment. They might not always feel like an active part in your life, but they can resurface when you experience something that brings back memories of your father's absence. Fears such as these need to be addressed head-on and require work to heal. Of course, you can heal from them too.

Remember the words of the Apostle Paul in 2 Timothy 1:7 (ESV),

"for God gave us a spirit not of fear but of power and love and self-control."

Master your fear through the power of the Holy Spirit. No longer allow fear to master you.

FEAR OF FAILURE

Everyone experiences a fear that they might fail from time to time. This only becomes an issue when that fear keeps us from becoming the men God has called us to be. God redeemed us to be grow in our faith and to have a grateful, willing heart to learn. Because your father's abandonment made you feel worthless and eroded your self-worth, directly or indirectly, you likely felt that him leaving was your fault and failure. You had no control however, and as a result you came to fear failure in general.

You rationalize that it is better to do nothing than it would be to try and fail.

It is possible that you have experienced the pain and embarrassment of failure enough times that it has deepened this belief. This is a key area to pivot your perspective today. Don't fear failure. Embrace failure and learn from it. A good and present father would have taught you that. His absence instead taught you the opposite, that your failure pushed him away.

Another lie!

Overcoming fear requires you to experience and recognize the "wins" in your life with abiding gratitude, and to have the proper focus on what is most important. First, your focus needs to be on becoming the man God created you to be - the Pastor, Provider, Protector and a man who imitates Christ Jesus in all things. This may sound daunting but keep your eyes on becoming *that* man and remember that you have the Holy Spirit and your brothers in Christ to help you.

Second, we all need to experience the momentum of cumulative biblical wins in life. This builds confidence and battles the fear of failure. The best way to do this is by stacking little wins together and understanding how this works progressively towards a worthy goal bringing glory to Jesus. There are so many if you dare to look and understand.

Every breath, every smile, every sunrise is a glorious gift!

How do you climb a mountain? One step at a time.

In the context of your role as a godly man, husband, and father, a little win could be as simple as committing to pray with your wife or kids for five minutes on five days during the week. Set the time and days and then do it. If you miss a day, then just re-evaluate why it was missed and tweak your routine for greater success. As you experience this win, select another area and goal to work on, perhaps in how you provide for your family. Achieve that win and select another.

We never fully arrive at in this fallen world, but we can complete fully all the work God has prescribed us to do. The Lord takes great joy in our intent, our effort, and our commitment to developing towards the man we should be in Christ. Both you and your family will thrive as a result of these grateful, biblically focused wins.

Throughout this process, your small wins will become larger wins and you will overcome the abiding sense of failure since you are a new creation in Christ.

NOT BEING LIKED

You are not alone in struggling with the desire to have people like you. This problem often starts with the belief you are not valuable. God created you with specific plans in mind and with a desire to see you conformed to the likeness of Jesus. You are priceless!

The hard truth is that there will *always* be people who don't like you. That does not change the value God has placed on you. We are called to be "kind", not liked by this world.

Even your father was wrong about your worth. If you regularly fail in your commitments, even little promises, and people don't like you because you're unreliable, *become* reliable because that honors God - not just to please others. Do you see the pattern here? If people don't like you because of your sin or foolishness, then work on those areas because it is not who God created you to be.

Sadly, way too many men are not "Promise Keepers". They say yes to things, not to offend, or to avoid someone being disappointed without earnestly trying to fulfill that promise. It gets back to the original sin of Adam.

The Obsession with "Likes"

You have to be discerning. Who doesn't like you, and why?

Even if it might feel good, is it important, useful, or valuable to be liked by everyone? What would *that* say about you? It is a natural conflict. You probably shouldn't be liked by people who fundamentally oppose your values. You'll have to prepare yourself that when you become a man of

God, fully righteous in that image, that you'll become less likable to some people. Misery loves company. Sinners gravitate to one another. I say, even as we want to be liked, and crave love, we should also be *unlikable* to those who do not share God's vision and values! If people don't like you *without* good reasons, or especially if they don't like you because you're following the Lord's direction and biblical principles for your life, then you have to remind yourself about what God values most and not worry about these other people.

BEING OUT OF CONTROL

What is control? Understanding what that means for you will be helpful in determining what makes you feel out of control.

This fear is common for boys and men who were left by their fathers. It's a fear that creates stress and anxiety that, left unresolved, can be crippling. Your dad was not in the home to protect the family. That created a vacuum that sucked safety and security from the home. To create a safer environment, you either fought for control over people and situations or you lived amidst the stress and anxiety of an unsafe environment. This sense of environmental chaos is easily picked up by a person. You might fear losing control of your own emotions, actions, etc. Feeling like your environment is out of control feeds the fear of losing whatever control you have.

Stop and evaluate the situation in which you most often feel a fear of losing control.

Is it related to your father's absence? If the answer is "yes," stop and ask if this fear is keeping you from forgiving him and/or being more like Jesus. Do you really *need* to have control in this situation? Is the fear rational and genuinely related to being unsafe? Do you fear that others will harm you or those you love?

Face and deal with this fear by asking good questions and deciding if it fits with who God has made you to be.

THE HELPLESSNESS OF INSECURITY

Insecurity develops when long periods of feeling worthless meet personal doubt. Insecurity causes you to feel a lack of certainty and confidence in who you are and about your decisions. It can also lead to depression. The absence of your father was traumatic and caused you to feel worthless, to doubt your choices and direction, or both.

The longer that you avoid addressing this feeling, the more hopeless and darker your life will feel.

Start by identifying the causes of your insecurity. What is making you feel worthless and causing you to doubt your choices? Do you over compensate for this insecurity? The chances are that it goes back to your relationship with your father and his absence from your life.

Overcoming this sense of insecurity requires you to change your focus from yourself to God and the wonderful plan He has for you. Follow the advice of Jesus,

> *"Seek first the kingdom of God and his righteousness, and all these things will be added to you. Therefore, do not be anxious about tomorrow, for tomorrow will be anxious for itself. Sufficient for the day is its own trouble."* Matthew 6:33-34 (ESV)

Work on today. You cannot change yesterday. Tomorrow can be taken care of when it gets here. A general rule about understanding depression is when one obsesses with the past. Anxiety, in general, is when one obsesses about the future. God has created you to do Kingdom work with Him. The Holy Spirit lives in you to help you do this work.

As we discussed before, stack small biblical wins. Winning is a skill formed by consistent discipline. It is a muscle that you develop over time, building confidence.

As you see those gains, belief in yourself through trust in Christ will combat the feeling of helplessness, or lack of confidence, and can help control both anxiety and insecurity.

DESPAIR

Despair is defined as the *complete* loss or absence of hope, disheartenment, discouragement, desperation, distress, anguish, depression, misery, defeatism, pessimism, and even suicidal feelings.

I keep reminding you that God sees you as priceless and has an intentional part for you play in the Kingdom, but when you are in the pit of despair these truths ring hollow and feel empty. It is easy to hear and come to believe the voice of the enemy saying, "You're worthless. God could never love you or use you." These lies need to be overcome so that you can experience the full life you have in Christ.

The Apostle Paul tells believers that every aspect of their life is to be lived to the glory of God that others would see their actions and glorify God. This is a tall order! To accomplish this, he tells them,

> *"Do not be conformed to this world, but be transformed by the renewal of your mind, that by testing you may discern what is the will of God, what is good and acceptable and perfect."* Romans 12:2 (ESV)

I love how this charter focuses on something you can I can actively do. This means that you shouldn't allow the world or the Devil to dictate what you believe. Instead, allow the Holy Spirit to transform your mind to learn how to please God with your life.

Trust your Abba Father.

Do you believe God *can*?

Can He lift your despair? Can He reframe the context and write a wholly new chapter in your life? Can He equip and strengthen you? Can He go before you and protect you?

If you <u>do</u> believe that He can do all these things and more, then become a man of action and <u>act</u> like it!

Now, an even more profound question for you. Do you believe He *will*? I'd argue that you have something to say and do with that. God's promises are often conditional on our behavior. Call it a holy partnership.

Your father's absence was terrible and caused despair from his betrayal, but that is no longer who you are in Christ. When you hear these lies call them out for what they are. Remember, those voices you hear are either from the Lord or from Satan. Before we act on it or believe it true about ourselves, the first step is to discern who is it from. Discernment can only come from reading and believing what God says is true about you from His Word, the Bible. If you do not become disciplined in practice of opening your Bible to read God's Truth about you, you will continue to struggle with the little voice in your head.

Remind yourself that God will continue to perfect the good work He began in you when you came to faith. The Apostle Paul put it this way,

> *"I am sure of this, that he who began a good work in you will bring it to completion at the day of Jesus Christ."* Philippians 1:6 (ESV).

Despair should be replaced with the hope you have in Christ for salvation and the realization that God has great plans for you. His plans should not be thwarted!

FEELING UNWORTHY

Feeling unworthy is best described as a battle for your self-value. God has told you, His adopted son, that you are priceless and worthy of love. After all, He died for your sins to give you eternal life. The struggle with unworthiness comes because it is a challenge for us to replace our ideas of what is valuable about us with God's ideas.

What does the perfect *you* look like in your own mind?

Write down a list of what you believe success and value looks like in you. Now compare those definitions with the following passages in Scripture that describe how God considers your value:

John 1:12; 15:5, 15; Romans 8:1, 16-17, 28, 37; 12:2; 1 Corinthians 3:16; 6:19-20; 12:27; 2 Corinthians 2:14; 5:17-19; Galatians 2:20; 3:26-28, 36; Ephesians 2:10; Philippians 1:6; Colossians 3:3, 12; 2 Timothy 1:7; 1 Peter 2:9

How does your list today compare to how you thought about your worth and self-value when you were young? When you compare your list to God's perspective you will notice that *your* criteria are probably nearly impossible to live up to. By contrast, the Lord's list is what He has already done for you and is doing *through* you.

Not only does He hold you in great esteem and value, He *gave* you that very value!

Albeit a habit, the best way to practically deal with feeling unworthy is to be disciplined about reminding yourself about how valuable you are to God and to ask the Holy Spirit to reveal these truths to you daily. If battling the feelings of unworthiness has been a lifelong challenge, change won't come overnight but change will come.

Begin that journey and be encouraged because you're not alone. Finally, remember that you're not making a change to become worthy. You already are. You're simply changing your belief in your God-given worthiness and daily habits your flesh does not want to let go of without a fight.

STRIVING FOR PERFECTION

As a child, perfectionist tendencies stemmed from a belief that if you excelled and were amazing, your father will love you and triumphantly return.

As you grew and matured, it assumes that you could be so successful that he would have no choice but to be proud of you and change his ways. Setting the goal to be perfect will lead you to unhappiness and frustration, because no one is perfect, except God (Matthew 5:48; 10:18). Expecting perfection is setting yourself up for failure. Perfectionism can make you very difficult to be around because your quest for perfection will bleed over to your expectations of others. It is very frustrating to spend time with someone whose expectations are so high that you feel like a constant failure.

As such, perfectionists often find themselves alone. Frankly, perfectionism is the idol we worship. It is ok to fail as we learn.

Christ is perfect, and we are under His Lordship and already sees us as perfect.

The Self-Fulfilling Prophesy

You're so accustomed to being disappointed, you may even unconsciously set unrealistic goals and standards knowing that you cannot achieve them.

Hey, at least the failure is consistent and familiar, right? In reality, this self-defeating symptom comes from the same place as the insecurity, despair, and unworthiness. The instability in your early life did not allow you to build appropriate self-worth that was based on and affirmed by realistic expectations. And as such, the expectations pendulum has swung too far the opposite way.

The concept of perfection is a dichotomy because the Bible does indeed tell Believers that we are to *strive* to be perfect as God is perfect (Matthew 5:48). This is not because we *can* become perfect (this side of Heaven). The objective here is to establish the goal to be as Christ-like as possible, while realizing that, ultimately, we will fall short to keep our eyes on Jesus and not our works.

The striving itself focuses our attention and effort on the things Christ loves. It is a worthy target, not for perfectionism itself, but for the drive to perpetually model Jesus' perfection to become imitators of God (Ephesians 5:1) even in our failures when we ask for forgiveness. This place that is not our home, as such, a big part of that imitation is our willingness and quickness in asking for and granting forgiveness in our daily witness to the lost and broken world.

The difference between striving to imitate God's perfection and striving for *our* version of perfection is that our version stems from our own sinful nature. When you, a sinful person, set a human standard for perfection and then demand that of yourself and others, you are creating idols. Idols are distractions from God's standard. One idol is a behavioral pursuit of flawlessness for affirmation, (look what I can do), and the other is an idol of self-worship, (look how great I am!).

As with all idols in our lives, these require that we tear them down, repent, and return to worshiping the Lord alone.

Only when you see the truth of perfectionism for what it is can you begin to heal.

| Chapter 9: Study |

NEXT STEPS: Working through the chapter

    a. Evaluating how my emotions keep me from forgiving my earthly father:

    I am angry at my father for...

- My father's absence has left me lonely; I wish he had been there to...
- My hatred looks like...
- I am afraid of...

    b. My father was gone, he never saw/came to (*experiences*) with me and I am not sure how to forgive him for the hurt that caused.

GET ROLLING with the <u>Companion Guide</u>: Preparation to write a *Forgiveness Letter*:

- Utilize the *Man Enough to Forgive* Personal Study Journal workbook

| Scripture References |

1. From the Lord's perspective, hating others is as bad as killing them. Matthew 5:21-22 (NASB)

2. We cannot hate. We must love our brothers, even to the point of laying down our lives for one another. 1 John 3:15-16 (ESV).

3. God tells us not to fear. He gives us the power to love and have self-control. 2 Timothy 1:7 (ESV)

4. Seek first God's kingdom. Don't worry about tomorrow or be anxious. Matthew 6:33-34 (ESV)

5. Don't be conformed to this world. Seek the Lord's will for your life. Romans 12:2 (ESV)

6. Be confident! God will complete his work in you if you stay faithful. Philippians 1:6 (ESV)

7. What does God think about you? You have tremendous value in the Lord's eyes! John 1:12; 15:5, 15; Romans 8:1, 16-17, 28, 37; 12:2; 1 Corinthians 3:16; 6:19-20; 12:27; 2 Corinthians 2:14; 5:17-19; Galatians 2:20; 3:26-28, 36; Ephesians 2:10; Philippians 1:6; Colossians 3:3, 12; 2 Timothy 1:7; 1 Peter 2:9 All Scriptures (NASB)

8. No one is perfect but God. Matthew 5:48; 10:18 (NASB)

9. We should strive to be imitators of God's perfection, though we'll never be perfect. Ephesians 5:1 (NASB)

The Man God Intended You to Be

SERIES FOUR

Men Desire a Challenge

Will You Complete Your Promise?

sacrifice

[sac·ri·fice] **noun**

Motivated by faith in God and with an attitude that is pleasing to God. Conforming to our example in Christ Jesus.

CHAPTER TEN

Following Jesus – Forgiving Your Father

*"The Lord is slow to anger and abundant in loving kindness, **forgiving** iniquity and transgression; but He will by no means clear the guilty, visiting the iniquity of the **fathers** on the children to the third and the fourth generations."*
Numbers 14:18 (NASB)

| Quick Start |

Forgiveness comes from a place of humility that is born from experiencing God's love and the full realization that we don't deserve it.

This humility is a reflection of us loving God back. The Lord tells us to love our neighbor and even go so far as to love our enemy, just as He does. We are to extend the love and forgiveness we receive from the Heavenly Father to them.

Forgiveness is a clear mark identifying your mature Christian manhood.

Your earthly father hurt you and you might even harbor hatred for him, but God commands you to forgive him. This can be difficult to accept and challenging to do. Remember though that the Lord is not asking you to do anything that you're not capable of or that He Himself does not already do. Forgiveness is a requirement for receiving forgiveness from God. Jesus tells us,

> *"For if you forgive others their trespasses, your heavenly Father will also forgive you, but if you do not forgive others their trespasses, neither will your Father forgive your trespasses."* (Matthew 6:14-15).

There is a direct connection between our faithful obedience and genuine forgiveness of others and the forgiveness we can expect in return from God. Forgiveness extends mercy to the one who has committed the offense and allows faithful, obedient love to replace your anger, your desire for earthly justice, and temptation to pursue vengeance.

All of which give God the glory and points people to Him.

God not only commands Believers to practice forgiveness but He modeled this by sending His only Son to die on the cross for His adopted children. Jesus' penultimate act on the cross was to forgive those who crucified Him, even while he was in ultimate physical and emotional pain. While suffering from the asphyxiation caused by crucifixion, not to mention having been beaten throughout the night and scourged by the Romans that very morning, Jesus forgave the Roman soldiers.

> *Jesus prayed, "Father, forgive them."* (Luke 23:34).

He could have reigned down righteous judgement upon them, but He forgave them and further demonstrated his general love for all of His creation, despite their sin. Considering that we are called to model Jesus, and surely our pain and wounds do not compare to those He bore, how can we *not* forgive those who wrong us?

Because of your new life in Christ, you have experienced the amazing forgiveness of God and the indwelling Holy Spirit empowers and guides you to forgive. Without the power of the Holy Spirit it would be impossible for us to shed our earthly obstacle in order to truly forgive.

Even those wrongs we have defined as the unforgiveable sin.

Forgiveness removes the thirst for vengeance whether or not you can be reconciled. This is an individual act in which the injured person chooses to imitate God by extending the forgiveness we experienced in Christ Jesus to others.

Reconciliation, on the other hand, takes two or more people; The injured person(s) and the perpetrator(s) must come together. The person responsible for the damage must acknowledge their sin, repent specifically of that sin, and ask for forgiveness from those they injured. The wounded person(s) must extend forgiveness through the power of Christ in them.

Reconciliation does not mean you have to have a relationship with the offender. An important concept many confuse.

Forgiveness can be granted without reconciliation, but reconciliation cannot happen without forgiveness.

Many of the people we forgive will never be reconciled to us. They may not see their actions as wrong or harmful and refuse not only to repent but to seek reconciliation. It is tragic, but lack of reconciliation *cannot* be a reason *not* to forgive.

By committing from your heart to forgive your earthly father, you will begin to feel alive again. As I released my unforgiveness of my earthly father for abandoning me, my sister, and my mom, my soul was finally able to breath.

You can achieve freedom from the bitterness, anger, depression, anxiety, perfectionism, and lack of purpose in your life. This change is generally not instantaneous, but it *starts* immediately and grows more permanent as your wounds heal. Like getting gravel in a wound that then become infected, the hurts you received were festering and could not heal until they were completely removed. Each sin against you that you forgive removes a piece of gravel from the wound. Even as you clean the wound with forgiveness, it still takes time and attention to heal.

With your wound clean and healing, you can begin to see and fully experience the new life in Christ that God's grace has given you. You will have a deeper desire to know your Heavenly Father intimately and learn what it will take for you personally to be conformed to the image of Christ. You will desire to be more like Jesus and, maybe, but not necessary, to be reconciled with your earthly father - or just to be free from the bondage of unforgiveness. A cycle breaker.

You can truly be the man God intended you to be.

Forgive your earthly father and ask the Holy Spirit to help you write the forgiveness letter. Pray for your father if he is still alive.

| Road Map |

Forgiveness comes from a place of deep, soul transformation that has experienced the love of God with the full realization that we don't deserve it.

This transformation leads us to grow in our faithful, obedient love of God. Loving God requires us to love our neighbor and even go so far as to love our enemy, extending the love and forgiveness of God to them.

Your earthly father hurt you and you might even harbor hatred for him, but God commands you to obediently forgive him. This is a hard truth to hear, but remember God is not asking you to do anything He Himself does not already do. Again, it is not a suggestion, but a command.

Jesus Teaches Forgiveness

Forgiveness needs to flow from a place of personal humility and a desire to be in fellowship with our Father, then to our neighbor, and even to our enemies.

Humility by definition is a "modest opinion or estimate of one's own importance, rank, etc." You are a sinner, saved by the grace of God in Christ. You were unable in your own power to achieve perfection, let alone the rebirth of a new heart of flesh, the forgiveness of sin or the conquering of death.

> *"Moreover, I will give you a new heart and put a new spirit within you; and I will remove the heart of stone from your flesh and give you a heart of flesh."* Ezekiel 36:26 (NASB)

Humility recognizes that you, like the rest of humanity, needed to be saved by Christ.

Even as Believers, none of us is perfect or better than another in the eyes of our Heavenly Father. Rather, Believers are all one in Christ Jesus and need each another in the body of Christ.

<u>When we are humbled by the Righteous of Christ, you will be enabled to forgive.</u>

When Jesus was asked to summate what God's requires of His people, He replied,

> *"You shall love the Lord your God with all your heart and with all your soul and with all your mind. This is the great and first commandment. And a second is like it: You shall love your neighbor as yourself. On these two commandments depend all the Law and the Prophets."* (Matthew 22:37-40).

Throughout His ministry, Jesus used parables to illustrate God's expectations for human forgiveness. In Matthew 18:15-20 Jesus instructs the disciples to lead their brothers from sin to repentance and then to forgive them that the church might remain healthy. Peter asked Jesus how many *times* he should forgive his brother.

A simple and practical question, right?

Jesus' answer was so... well, so Jesus. Instead of giving Peter number, a minimum "rule" for the number of times one should reasonably forgive, he told the parable of the unforgiving servant (Matthew 18:23-35). This taught that we should have *no limits* to our forgiveness *and* that we will draw the Lord's discipline and fellowship consequences if we do not extend forgiveness to others when we have been forgiven our own debts/sins.

In the gospel of Luke, we are told five forgiveness parables: the barren fig tree (13:6-9); the bent over woman (13:10-13); the lost sheep (15:4-7); the lost coin (15:8-10); and the prodigal son (15:11-32). In each parable it highlights the need for forgiveness we have and how God dispenses forgiveness.

Jesus told His disciples,

> *"For if you forgive others their trespasses, your heavenly Father will also forgive you, but if you do not forgive others their trespasses, neither will your Father forgive your trespasses."*
> Matthew 6:14-15 (NASB).

This statement is linked to the Lord's Prayer, in which Jesus teaches his disciples *how* to pray. The Lord's Prayer is Jesus' "shout out loud" instructions, the most direct how-to for connecting with the Heavenly Father. We'd be wise to pay extra attention to the praise elements, the appeal elements, and the to the conditional nature of our request for forgiveness.

In that prayer, Jesus directs us to ask God to forgive our sins *in the exact same way* we forgive other people. This reiterates the link between our acts of forgiveness and the forgiveness we can expect in return from God. Forgiveness is connected to love and Heavenly Fellowship, as God instructs us to "love your neighbor as yourself."

> *"You shall not hate your brother in your heart, but you shall reason frankly with your neighbor, lest you incur sin because of him. You shall not take vengeance or bear a grudge against the sons of your own people, but you shall love your neighbor as yourself."*
> Leviticus 19:17-18 (ESV)

Imitating Christ – Forgiveness in Action

Do as I say *and* as I do.

Jesus did not merely teach about the need for forgiveness, He modeled it for us.

I'll begin by looking at the humility of Jesus, since it is here that forgiveness flows. In Jesus, we see the eternal Son Incarnate as a human being; fully God and fully man simultaneously. It would have been very easy for Jesus to destroy His enemies. Rather, He submitted to the Father and humbled Himself for the sake of His sheep that we might be saved from our sins.

The Apostle Paul points to this very fact in Philippians 2:5-12. Paul notes that Christ humbled Himself even to the point of death on a cross, the ultimate humiliation, not because He lacked power but *because* He wielded ultimate power. Christ modeled humility to its most extreme level because it is the harbinger for forgiveness. He had the right to destroy, but showed *restraint* and *unearned grace, sacrificial* humiliation, and *patience* knowing that the time of the Heavenly Father's ultimate justice will come. He knew that eventually those who wronged Him would witness His true power, but He resisted the urge to crush their arrogance.

We would be wise to model this behavior even in the small ways we can in our own daily lives. Again, our purpose is to bring Him glory and enjoy Him forever.

Throughout His ministry, Jesus modeled forgiveness from God's perspective by forgiving the sins of wretched sinners. He forgave His adopted children's sins that they would experience the mercy and love of God.

In Mark 2:5 he told the paralytic, *"My son, your sins are forgiven"* and then healed the man's physical ailments.

The spiritual need for forgiveness of sins was the man's greater need, and thus the miracle performed first. Luke 7:37-50 recounts Jesus eating with Simon the Pharisee when a sinful woman anointed Jesus' feet with alabaster oil and her tears. Jesus recognized her faith-filled humility and forgave her sins.

He points out to Simon that the bigger the debt the more grateful the one forgiven. In John 8:1-11, Jesus uses the situation of a woman who was caught in the sin of adultery to help the people see their own hypocritical view of sin. With her authentic repentance, Jesus then forgave the woman's sin and admonished her to stop her sinful activities. It's never too late for a turnaround!

Even as He hung on the cross, Jesus forgave the sins of the thief hanging next to Him once he believed and repented. (Luke 23:32:43).

Proof Positive He Was God in Man

This demonstrated forgiveness by Jesus was poured out on those who crucified Him. There is no other better example. After having been beaten throughout the night and scourged by the Romans, suffering from the asphyxiation caused by crucifixion, Jesus forgave the Roman soldiers.

Jesus prayed, *"Father, forgive them."* (Luke 23:34). Too often we are unable to see past our own personal hurts and desire for vengeance to forgive. Yet here we see the limitless length Jesus was willing to go to show us the power of forgiveness and guide us towards modeling His ways. He IS the example to follow.

As the Apostle Paul reminded the Ephesians Believers, we are to *"Be kind to one another, tenderhearted, forgiving one another, as God in Christ forgave you."* (Ephesians 4:32).

The Holy Spirit Empowers Us to Forgive

As a Christian, you have experienced the amazing forgiveness of God in Christ and this experience is the first step to being able to forgive others.

But guess what? You're human and in a daily battle with your flesh. Forgiving, especially something as deep seated and crushing as abandonment, is hard! But being hard is not an excuse. It typically means it is the right thing to do.

God knows and He's covered that too. The Heavenly Father promised to send help (beyond your ability) from the Holy Spirit, the third person of the Trinity, who abides in you to empower and guide you. We see this first when the risen Christ is meeting with the disciples.

> *"Jesus said to them again, 'Peace be with you. As the Father has sent me, even so I am sending you.' And when he had said this, He breathed on them and said to them, 'Receive the Holy Spirit. If you forgive the sins of anyone, they are forgiven; if you withhold forgiveness from anyone, it is withheld.'"* John 20:21-23 (ESV)

Again, you're never alone and the seemingly impossible is possible with God. The power to forgive is given to us because of our new life in God through Christ and the indwelling Spirit.

> *"I can do all things through Him who strengthens me."*
> Philippians 4:13 (ESV)

Forgiveness is truly an act of God through us by means of the Holy Spirit. On our own we choose to harbor the desire for vengeance over forgiveness, but through the power of God that changes our heart. We put our selfish, fleshly desires aside that we might "be perfect as God is perfect" and that we might honor Him as we forgive as He forgives.

Matthew 18:23-35 tells us that it is through bold understanding how our Heavenly Father has forgiven us that we can extend this forgiveness to others. When we gratefully acknowledge the large debt paid on our behalf by Christ on the cross, we can press on to forgive the relatively small debts of others.

We must have the courage and clarity to recognize our debts in their fullness through the power of the Holy Spirit in our lives (John 16:7-11).

Forgiveness vs. Reconciliation

Forgiving others' sin or offenses is not the same as reconciliation. (<u>Please note this vital point since our society, even well-meaning pastors confuse the two</u>.)

The spirit of true forgiveness communicates,

> "You have harmed me, but I will not seek vengeance or allow this hurt to define me. I will not hold this evil against you because I do

not want God to hold my evil against me. It will be a challenge to release my claim on offense, and I may be reminded of scars or the hurt. However, I will not let a healed scar break open and become a festering wound."

In the book of Genesis, Joseph stands as a great example of hardcore biblical forgiveness. His brothers *sold him into slavery*. But later in life when the tables had turned and Joseph had an opportunity to take vengeance upon his brothers, instead, he showed them grace and mercy. He had forgiven their treachery years before they came to him to ask for forgiveness and he did not allow false righteousness to undo that forgiveness.

When Joseph's brothers realized they stood before the very man they sold and discarded, they feared his judgement and wrath - and why wouldn't they? But instead of the condemnation and punishment they expected and deserved, they were shown a level of grace that can only be extended if forgiveness has been granted. Joseph had every "legal" right to burn them good; to teach them a painful lesson. In fact, in that day and time no one would have blamed Joseph for that reaction. However, Joseph had God's power within him. He was more than a mere man with the right to retribution. Only his forgiveness could have borne witness to others the supernatural power of the Heavenly Father in Joseph.

That alone was counter cultural and shocking. What a witness for the generations.

Forgiveness, for us too, impacts more than the two parties. Everyone around those involved are impacted and see the radical change and influence of faith in the One True God. It shines brightly and honors Jesus as we, even in our imperfect humanity, seek to emulate His life. It was Joseph's *humbling* mercy that allowed the brothers to reconcile. Through Joseph's example, his brothers were shaken from their arrogant and evil ways and they *asked* for forgiveness even though Joseph had already done so.

True forgiveness takes seeking vengeance off the table, even without consideration if or when reconciliation will occur. This is an individual activity in which the injured person, through the power of the Holy Spirit, must commit to imitate God by extending the forgiveness we experienced in Christ Jesus to others.

Reconciliation, on the other hand, takes two or more people. The injured person(s) and the perpetrator(s) must come together. One must repent, acknowledge his sin, take full responsibility for it, and ask for forgiveness from the other. Then, the injured person(s) must extend forgiveness.

Many of the people we forgive will never be reconciled to us. They may not see their actions as wrong or harmful and refuse to repent or seek reconciliation. Or sometimes, the other person is simply unreachable or has passed away. It is tragic to be denied this additional healing, but the lack of reconciliation or fear of reconciliation cannot be a reason *not* to forgive. The lost world so desperately needs to see Jesus in and through us as His witness.

If God had waited to forgive *us* until *we* repented and until we did our part for full reconciliation with Him, all of humanity would be going to Hell. Our wretched selfishness would keep us from God permanently. As we consider Jesus' life and His perfection as both man and God, we see the vast difference between our lives and true Holiness. It is in Jesus' death and resurrection that we can truly see the purpose and impact of forgiveness.

It should be highly motivating to us and inspire a desire for grace and mercy that drives us towards repentance, reconciliation, and restored Fellowship with Him and others.

Like with Joseph's brothers, your change of heart and faith-in-action, along with your obedient and proactive act of "being first" to forgive may be a shocking, unexpected, and a radical pivot point that catalyzes change in your father's heart and mind. Then you allow the Holy Spirit to finish the change and work in him.

The letter of forgiveness that you write and deliver to your earthly father might be the first and best example of real Christian grace that your earthly father ever receives - such a profound act in this broken and selfish world that is not our home.

Being Set Free from the Sin of Unforgiveness

God created us: mind, body, and soul. When any one of these parts suffer, the rest suffer with it.

If you have unconfessed sin, it will not just affect your soul but will begin to harm both your body and your mind through the broken fellowship with the Lord.

King David stands as a great example of this. After having sex with *his friend* Uriah's wife, David had his friend killed and married Bathsheba. From these terrible sins, everything in David's life went downhill (2 Samuel 11-12). In Psalm 32 David recounted how his bones were wasting away because he refused to confess and deal with his sin. His unconfessed sin was destroying him from within. Remember, this is King David we're talking about here – one of God's most special and beloved men in all the Bible. If sin can dominate *David's* life for a period of time, if that unconfessed sin can rot *him* from within, and if he can repent and come clean to then be used by God in incredible ways – so too we can be tempted, repent and be forgiven, and be restored.

Remember, unforgiveness is a sin.

Like all sin, if unconfessed and unrepented for, the sin of unforgiveness will continue to slowly destroy us. When we confess our sin as David does in Psalm 32, we find the peace of God purifies and heals us.

By forgiving your earthly father and repenting before the Lord for harboring unforgiveness, you will begin to feel revived so your soul can deeply rest in the Lord's Sovereignty. Like taking a shower after a hard day of digging in the dirt, confessing sin is cleansing and refreshing.

Science has also proven the biophysical rewards of living as the Lord commands. The Mayo Clinic notes that when we forgive and let go of bitterness we experience the following:[1]

---

[1] https://www.mayoclinic.org/healthy-lifestyle/adult-health/in-depth/forgiveness/art-20047692

- Healthier relationships
- Improved mental health
- Less anxiety, stress and hostility
- Lower blood pressure
- Fewer symptoms of depression
- A stronger immune system
- Improved heart health
- Improved self-worth

In the previous chapter we discussed how God forgives and expects us to forgive. In His love for us, He desires for our body to be treated like a temple. To be used for worship, our body must be in good health and order. When looking at the effect of forgiveness on the whole person, it is no wonder God emphasizes the need for people to forgive and resist the desire for vengeance. Forgiveness sets your body, mind, and soul free from sin and the death it brings.

Here is the start of true life found in the new creation we are in Christ.

The Transforming Power of Forgiveness

Do you remember the person you were *before* you put your faith in Christ? The selfishness that drove your former life has been forgiven and replaced by the Holy Spirit and a desire to serve Christ. This came about by the power of God, the regeneration of your heart by the Holy Spirit prompting your confession of sin and repentance. Harboring unforgiveness towards your father is the old way of life and no longer reflects the reborn you - forgiven by Christ Jesus.

If the forgiveness you experienced changed you then you need to *believe* it **can** change your earthly father (if he is still alive).

When you forgive those who wrong you it honors God, it points the lost to Jesus, it changes you to be like Him, and most importantly, it restores Fellowship with your Heavenly Father.

The Good Shepherd Cares for the ONE

Why does the Heavenly Father even care about me? I'm only one boy, one man among billions and billions of His creations over thousands of years on earth. We are tiny specs of dust in a celestial hurricane of space and time.

Does God really care, and if so, why?

We're incapable of even conceiving the scope of the Lord's focus or His sovereign plan. He's God after all. But we must believe Him when He says, "I know every hair on your head. I created you for a tremendous purpose. I came so that you can have life and live it abundantly. And I died for you – despite your sin – because I don't want you to be separated from me for eternity."

Wow. And what can we give Him in return? What does He need? Absolutely nothing.

What does He want?

He desires that we return His love and follow His commands. In this way, we can honor Him. We accomplish this by committing to be like Him, by obeying Him, and by being steadfast in extending forgiveness–just like Him.

Learning to Live a Life that's been Healed by Christ

When we give, we receive. Obeying the Lord and forgiving those who have wronged you kickstarts the healing in you. When unforgiveness is harbored it eats away at us and keeps us from seeing ourselves the way God does. He sees your sins as forgiven. He sees you as His adopted child and an inheritor of the Kingdom of God (Romans 8:15; Ephesians 1:13-14; James 2:5; 1 Peter 3:7).

You can no longer live as you did when you were a slave to sin. You must "be Holy as He is Holy" (1 Peter 1:16) and this requires the ongoing forgiveness of others (Matthew 18:21-35). Remember what I said about developing spiritual muscle, biblical courage?

A New Meaning of Grace

With your heart unburdened by sin, you start to really understand the amazing gift of grace that given to us by God through Jesus Christ. In Chapter 4 of Hebrews, we are told that Christ is the High Priest who knows all of our trials and tribulations because He endured them in the flesh too. His grace is not given to us because of our merit, but because of His perfect and sinless life on earth.

The Son became man in order to heal and save us. This is just one example of the Heavenly Father's deep love for His adopted children. Love requires an object of affection. Always and forever the Father loves the Son and Spirit and vice versa.

Through salvation, that we are received but have not earned, we enter into this eternal love relationship. We are both an object of love and a lover, being actively molded into the image of the Son. Understanding this tenant of Christianity is life-changing, but it cannot be truly experienced until we confess, and bring to light our sin. Only then can we truly see how His death, the price He paid for our sins, allows us to experience the gift of eternal life with Him, and in the eternal Triune life of love.

That is how much our Heavenly Father loves us!

Accelerate Your Healing

To fuel healing and to help grow our forgiving spirit, we need to invest time each day reading the Word. We need to be in prayer and in fellowship with other Christians so we can better grasp who we are in Christ.

This should not be done in hopes of gaining additional favor or some reward from Christ. You already stand to inherit all He has inherited (Romans 8:17). Rather, you do these things to increase your awareness and understanding of everything God has given you, so that you can advance in your mission of becoming more like Jesus.

Christian men sharpen one another and build each other up – all for God's glory, and His alone.

Chapter 10: Study

NEXT STEPS: Working through the chapter

a. Why is forgiveness hard for you?

b. If God has forgiven your sins, what keeps you from forgiving yourself?

c. What stops you from extending forgiveness to your father?

d. What is keeping you from asking the Holy Spirit to help you obey God and forgive your earthly father?

e. Do you feel set free from the sin of unforgiveness? Why or why not?

f. What does "reconciliation" mean to you? What will that look like in your relationship with your father?

g. If you have not started the *Forgiveness Letter*, what is holding you back?

GET ROLLING with the <u>Companion Guide</u>: Preparation to write a *Forgiveness Letter*:

- Utilize the *Man Enough to Forgive* Personal Study Journal workbook

Scripture References

1. We are to imitate the forgiveness extended to us by Christ. Matthew 18:21-35 (NASB)

2. We are made in God's image and given dominion over all the earth's creatures. Genesis 1:26 (NASB)

3. A man is to leave his parents and join a woman in marriage, becoming one. Genesis 2:24 (NASB)

4. The Lord compares a man and woman's unity to the relationship between God and the Church. Ephesians 5:31-33 (NASB)

5. Man is not meant to separate from his wife and expect a smooth life. Malachi 2:16 (NASB)

6. We must have a limitless tank to forgiveness. We can't expect to be forgiven if we do not forgive. Matthew 18:21-35 (NASB)

7. Jesus told many parables about forgiveness. Here are 5 from the book of Luke: the barren fig tree (13:6-9); the bent over woman (13:10-13); the lost sheep (15:4-7); the lost coin (15:8-10); and the prodigal son (15:11-32) All NASB.

8. Jesus reiterates, to be forgiven one must forgive. Matthew 6:14-15 (NASB)

9. You should not hate, seek vengeance, or bear a grudge against others. Leviticus 19:17-18 (ESV)

10. Christ humbled Himself that we might be saved from our sins. Philippians 2:5-12 (NASB)

11. Jesus performed miracles for hurting people who had faith. Mark 2:5 (NASB)

12. Jesus forgave the sins of a scorned woman because she humbled herself and sought forgiveness. Luke 7:37-50 (NASB)

13. Jesus demonstrated it's never too late to turn around your life and seek forgiveness. John 8:1-11 (NASB)

14. Even unto death, Jesus was forgiving others. Luke 23:32:43 (NASB)

15. Jesus interceded on man's behalf asking the Heavenly Father to forgive man. Luke 23:34 (NASB)

16. Apostle Paul reminded the Ephesian people to be kind and forgive one another. Ephesians 4:32 (NASB)

17. Jesus brought the Holy Spirit to his disciples, and with Him, the encouragement to forgive. John 20:21-23 (ESV)

18. You can do all things in Christ, who strengthens you. Philippians 4:13 (ESV)

19. By understanding how we are forgiven, it helps us to forgive others. Matthew 18:23-35 (NASB)

20. We have to be honest in our evaluation of our sins and need for forgiveness. John 16:7-11 (NASB)

21. Because of King David's sins, his life went entirely downhill. 2 Samuel 11-12 (NASB)

22. In Psalms 32, David confesses mourns his sins. Psalm 32 (NASB)

23. God sees you as His adopted child and an inheritor of His Kingdom. Romans 8:15; Ephesians 1:13-14; James 2:5; 1 Peter 3:7 (NASB)

24. You can't live in sin as you did before. We're chartered to be holy as He is holy. 1 Peter 1:16 (NASB)

25. Christ is the High Priest who knows all of our trials and tribulations because He endured them in the flesh too. Hebrews, Chapter 4 (NASB)

26. We stand to inherit salvation, just as Jesus did. Romans 8:17 (NASB)

honor

[hon·or] **noun**

Our esteem and respect come when we honor God. We give Him reverence and homage, for God alone is worthy of our highest honor.

CHAPTER ELEVEN

Being the Man of God You Were Created to Be

"Now I praise you because you remember me in everything and hold firmly to the traditions, just as I delivered them to you. But I want you to understand that Christ is the head of every man, and the man is the head of a woman, and God is the head of Christ."
1 Corinthians 11:1-3 (NASB)

| Quick Start |

When God created Adam and Eve, He gave them specific roles in their relationship to one another, to the rest of the creation, and to the leadership roles within the family and within His church.

The rules He set were for their good and to ensure a grateful and healthy existence. Adam disobeyed Him and sin entered the world, throwing the Lord's design into chaos. As men, we need to recognize the role in the family God designed for us. Through the power of the Holy Spirit, we are to live out that purpose. We can only bring true healing to our families when we fulfill the role God created for us.

The lifeblood of the family is Christ's love we are to demonstrate. We are to focus on helping one another to honor God in all aspects of life. The husband and father should demonstrate the grace and mercy of God daily and work diligently to foster these same disciplines in family members. Each member of a family is to encourage and build one another up in the same way the church does.

As the leader and spiritual head of the household, the man is to act as a priest leading his family in faith, in worship, and in service. And, as we have been discussing, *man enough* to be the leader in the acts of forgiveness.

It Begins with You

You must be this type of leader in your home. This requires you to lead by example, not just by command. Your job is to lead your family, obeying the directions of Christ, which includes but is not limited to serving others, how to love, how to forgive, and how to extend mercy and grace to other people.

This becomes the driving force for a faithful man. You model Christ's behavior and are a present example for your family members of what it means to know Jesus and have the Holy Spirit transforming you into His image.

Finally, you need to break the cycle of abandonment and dysfunction in your family. This requires not only extending forgiveness to your earthly father, but actively and humbly seeking forgiveness from those who you have wronged. It is a powerful example of being Christ-like to forgive those who have wronged you and not to seek vengeance.

In a permissive and increasingly "anything goes" culture, it is vital that you demonstrate the strength of character evident when seeking forgiveness from others after falling short of Christ's standards especially to your family under your care.

BEING THE MAN GOD CREATED YOU TO BE MEANS IMITATING GOD'S LOVE <u>IN ACTIONS</u>.

| Road Map |

In the beginning, God created Adam, then Eve, and scripted for them unique roles and responsibilities so they could complement one another and bring glory to Himself. These roles for men extend to the small family and to the larger family within the church.

The family system was designed by God for our benefit as the perfect unit to sustain generations of people that will come from us. If His grand design is ignored, abandoned, excused away, broken or muddled, the results are devastating to everyone involved.

Understanding your God-given role provides a fulfilling blueprint for your life - one that should not be manipulated or perverted by the fluidity of culture around you. Follow God's design and you'll be the man God created you to be. Be God's man!

GOD'S DESIGN FOR THE FAMILY

In the actual and historical creation account, shared in the Book of Genesis, we learn that God created man and then created woman to complement him.

Make no mistake – men need complimenting. In His design, neither man nor woman are complete without the other. This is not to say that a man can't live in God's image without a wife and children, but that the family architecture of one man and one woman is perfect to the natural order and balance – especially if children are involved.

Men need women to be complete in their calling the same way that women needed men to pastor, provide and protect her (Genesis 2:20-25; 4:1). As a couple, God intends for the man and woman to become one person in body, mind and spirit (Genesis 2:24; Matthew 19:5).

This is why God hates divorce. It destroys the life created in the act of marriage because it divides one "body" back into two. And, in reality, it is broken into many pieces. The family functions properly when the husband

and wife commit to be one for the remainder of their lives and raise their children in the respect and reverent fear of the Lord (Proverbs 14:26-27). The home is meant to be the most peaceful, joyous, and secure learning environment for children.

Life in a family is one of love with a focus on spiritual life and the well-being of each other. The father is called to model the mercy and grace of our Lord Jesus and to coach and encourage the same in each member of the family.

> *"Likewise, husbands, live with your wives in an understanding way, showing honor to the woman as the weaker vessel, since they are heirs with you of the grace of life, so that your prayers may not be hindered. Finally, all of you, have unity of mind, sympathy, brotherly love, a tender heart, and a humble mind."* 1 Peter 3:7-8 (ESV)

Christian men are not just the leaders of the home (the small church), but the *physical* representation of Christ to the family in both word and deed. This is yet another important point that supports the urgent nature of being present in the home both for the benefit of children and spouse.

How can you be the physical representation of Christ if you are always away for work, away pursuing your time-consuming hobbies OR away because you have divorced and your kids do not live with you? You can't, no matter what the so-called modern culture trics to tell us.

Ephesians 6:1-4 directs that children are to honor and obey their parents and fathers are commanded not to "provoke [children] to anger" because then they will not only rebel against their earthly father but their Heavenly Father.

In many regards, the family operates like a small church. It functions to support and build up the spiritual walk of its members and to take the Gospel out into the community. In this same way, the father is the pastor of his flock and should mirror the qualifications for his role. Paul tells us the qualifications of a biblical man is to be:

> *"...above reproach, the husband of one wife, sober-minded, self-controlled, respectable, hospitable, able to teach, not a drunkard, not violent but gentle, not quarrelsome, not a lover of money. He must manage his own household well, with all dignity keeping his children submissive."* 1 Timothy 3:2-4 (ESV).

If the man leads by godly example, then his wife and children will be far more likely to respond in kind. The Word of God directs that wives must be devoted to their husbands and their children in the same way they are devoted to Christ. (Ephesians 5:22-23). If the husband does not emulate Christ, how can he expect His wife to? Or his children?

The Battle Over Submission

In the discussion of the biblical structure of marriage and guiding principles of a Christian family, few scriptures draw as much controversy as Ephesians 5:22-24 (ESV).

> *"Wives, submit to your own husbands, as to the Lord. For the husband is the head of the wife even as Christ is the head of the church, his body, and is himself its Savior. Now as the church submits to Christ, so also wives should submit in everything to their husbands."*

Why the controversy?

In the context of the Heavenly Father's direction of men and women in marriage, biblical submission means to respect, honor, love, serve, to be humble, and to be helpful. In all these ways, to be submissive to one's spouse is efficient and effective for a loving and productive relationship and family.

Again, God is not a liar.

As goes the marriage, so too will go the family. One cannot be sick and the other healthy. Whether or not you have a faithful disposition, humankind does not fare well in any communal structure *without* submission. The most important component of this call to submission is to recognize the

Lord's ultimate sovereignty above all else. We submit to Him, and we must submit elsewhere as He commands. His plan is perfect.

This is the reference point then for the marriage relationship and for the home, family life, and the church. It prescribes roles, responsibilities and a working authority tree. It does not declare that one party is better, of higher value to God, or more holy in His eyes. However, no family, no community, no church, no business, and no organization of two or more people can thrive without a defined leader. God has chosen those roles.

Anything, shy of some agreed upon order eventually devolves to chaos – every time.

This mantle of leadership can't and shouldn't be deferred, abandoned, or reassigned. For men to fail in their responsibility to the family through divorce or abandonment of their fatherly role represents a collapse of the privilege granted to them by God.

When your family functions as God created and commands it, you will find joy even in the midst of turmoil and sorrow. Growing up in a family that does not function this way leads to difficulty and dysfunction. The family takes its operational leadership cues from the man as he fulfills his sacred duties well.

The God created polarity of man's masculinity and a women's nurturing form and raise a healthy child and family unit.

MEN'S UNIQUE ROLES

A Sacred Challenge – And You Are Man Enough!

Leader:

As we examine family structure, proven over the millennia regardless of culture, race, worldview, or even time and technology, why is it that the nuclear family design of a man and wife with the children all together in the home is the <u>only</u> lasting recipe for successful families?

It is because it is God's perfect design.

The role of family leader comes with unique expectations. Scripture tells us that Adam was created first and charged with being the leader of the family. The New Testament takes this concept a step further as men are commanded to love their wife and children as Christ loves the Church. In Ephesians 5:17-33 Paul compares the life of the Church with the life of the family. While all Believers submit to Christ and act with faith-filled humility towards one another, wives submit to their husbands and in turn husbands cherish their wives as Christ cherishes all of Creation. This means we are required to be willing to lay down our life for our family and place their needs above our own.

There should be nothing we would *not do* and *no sacrifice* too great to uphold our responsibility as Pastor, Provider, and Protector.

This shoots a hole in our culture's wide acceptance of divorce simply for "irreconcilable differences," much less for commonly heard excuses like, "my spouse nags me," "I don't get sex enough,", "my kids are better off", or, "I'm just bored with marriage."

In 1 Corinthians Paul says it this way,

> "...I want you to understand that the head of every man is Christ, the head of a wife is her husband, and the head of Christ is God."

Make no mistake about it, your leadership role in the family begins with a very discerning process along with a God honoring decision in the choosing of the future mother of your children.

In the same way that Christ leads us as men, we need to lead our wives and children. This means actively reading God's Word with them and talking about how we are to try to be more Christ-like. We need to teach our family how to pray, and to show reverence and affection for God each day and in an ongoing way (1 Timothy 5:17). We lead by going to church and worshiping together to help them understand the tenants and practices of the Christian faith.

For your family to understand and submit to this perfect family order, and for you to lead as spiritual head of household, they need to know this model isn't some power grab on your behalf or your brilliant idea. This is another reason why it's so key to be reading Scripture together, and maturity in your relationship with the Heavenly Father. It will help your family understand the high standard you are being held to fulfill while submitting to God's authority, following His rules, and honoring His plan.

This will require you to be intentionally and actively growing in your own Christian faith.

Leadership of the family is a lifelong journey. Even after your children are grown, you will remain a key leader in their lives. Mentoring your grown children has different requirements than leading your younger children - but it is *still* your job.

To lead well you need to also be mastering and modeling the skills you teach and to live out a rich Christian life. Your family is learning as much or more by observing what you do. This is particularly risky if there is a disconnect between what you say and advocate and what you actually do.

But you're up for the challenge. As a leader, you have to be.

Model:

Since our families are watching us, we need to talk about the unique role men play in their families as a model of godly behavior.

In 1 Corinthians, Chapter 10, Paul addresses an issue that is dividing the church concerning their former way of worshiping and living out their new life in Christ. He carefully crafts his reasoning and concludes that they should be driven not only by a desire to imitate Christ but to place the needs of others above their own. He concludes this point in 1 Corinthians 11:1 by saying, *"Be imitators of me, as I am of Christ."* Paul is leading even as he offers himself as a model.

Here Paul expresses a deep truth that's been proven across the centuries – if we are to try and imitate Christ, we will have more success if we *also* have an earthly example to follow.

Today, while we are following Christ's biblical examples, learn about Jesus through the lessons seen in more mature and experienced Christians and with the help of the Holy Spirit, because we can't see Jesus in the flesh every day. We need an active, godly role model in our life to follow. Even if you did not have that example when you were growing up, you must be a leading role model for those God has placed under your care.

Does your life reflect Christ each day?

We *all* struggle to model His behavior consistently each day. But we cannot quit when we sometimes fail. Rather, we must learn from our failures and use them to motivate us to follow Christ even *more* each day whereby we are quick in asking for forgiveness. We are sinners who have been saved by grace, who are being actively molded into the likeness of Christ for the glory of God, empowered by the Holy Spirit. This process is like exercising each day. You need to build on the previous workout and commit to the process. Small fits of effort don't develop sustainable momentum.

That's why committing to following Christ each day as the foundation of your maturing lifestyle is so vital.

Servant:

Even as the family's leader, boss, teacher, and motivator you are also called to serve others.

How we use our time and talents to serve God will be an example to our family. It is the man's job to model Christ, to serve Him, and to be of service to others while teaching his wife and children to do the same. One of the great examples of being a servant leader is Saint Nicholas, the Bishop of Myra in the 4th Century, better known as the original Santa Claus. Nicholas read Matthew 25:31-46 and took the words of Jesus to heart.

The Final Judgment

"When the Son of Man comes in his glory, and all the angels with him, then he will sit on his glorious throne. Before him will be gathered all the nations, and he will separate people one from another as a shepherd separates the sheep from the goats. And he will place the sheep on his right, but the goats on the left. Then the King will say to those on his right, 'Come, you who are blessed by my Father, inherit the kingdom prepared for you from the foundation of the world.

For I was hungry and you gave me food, I was thirsty and you gave me drink, I was a stranger and you welcomed me, I was naked and you clothed me, I was sick and you visited me, I was in prison and you came to me.'

Then the righteous will answer him, saying, 'Lord, when did we see you hungry and feed you, or thirsty and give you drink? And when did we see you a stranger and welcome you, or naked and clothe you? And when did we see you sick or in prison and visit you?'

And the King will answer them, 'Truly, I say to you, as you did it to one of the least of these my brothers, you did it to me.'"

In this section of Scripture, Christ is describing God judging and separating people for Heaven or Hell based on their saving faith. Those who trust in Christ for salvation serve Him by taking care of the poor, visit those in prison, invite in the stranger, protect the widow and fatherless, and care for those in need without thought of themselves. They imitate Jesus, for whom the sake of us sinners became man, suffered and died on our behalf that we might live forever with Him.

Heaven was their reward, but their joy was the selfless caring for others on earth in the name of Jesus.

St. Nicholas realized that since he belonged to Christ he needed to serve all people – just like as Christ did. He generously gave to the needy around him, often at night, anonymously and without earthly recognition. He loved others above himself because he had experienced this same love from Christ. The Scripture passage in Matthew did not scare Nicholas into service. Rather, it inspired him to serve others like Jesus did. In Nicholas' story we see the meaning of manly servanthood. We witness the strength and joy of being used by God in a powerful way. We should do the same.

The world needs us, men, to step up *right now* and *right away*. We should champion the poor, oppressed, imprisoned, fatherless, widowed, etc. because we follow the Servant King. And as men, we are commissioned to teach the same principles to our families.

Forgiver:

The role of men is one of great responsibility and fraught with peril, but it is tempered with the amazing reward of leading others in honoring God with their lives.

In all this we are reminded that we are not perfect, we still sin, but we are forgiven by God in Christ and that is life changing. So as men we lead and model and serve and we demonstrate forgiveness in all we do. Our wives and children learn how to forgive and are encouraged to do so by our acts of forgiveness.

When we are harmed, the former man in us wants vengeance. The world even encourages us to lash out, to "get yours" and to fight back. However, the new man that we are in Christ demands us to be counter-cultural and offer forgiveness instead. The Bible provides additional practical guidance. If you are harmed by someone publicly then you should forgive them publicly. If they harmed you in the past, forgive them in the present.

What is Most Important?

Elevate the salvation of the person whom you need to forgive above your desire for retribution or the satisfaction of your pride.

Yes, I know, people will say this is hard. Hard is never a reason or excuse as to why we should not do something, specially an instruction of the Lord's. A better word, a better way to think about it is, "saying it is sacrificial".

As Christ hung on the cross, He could have called armies of supporters in Heaven and on earth to avenge or save Him, but rather He prayed, *"Father, forgive them, for they know not what they do"* (Luke 23:34). Our Savior, our best example of how to live, forgave the offenses of others so they may find salvation. We can do nothing less and still call ourselves His people.

Genuine forgiveness is a mark of being a Christ follower.

This process of forgiving our father extends to asking for forgiveness when we wrong others. Even for those who generally take their role as a godly man, husband, and father seriously, this can be particularly challenging. It can feel like a reversal of the position as leader - like an erosion of strength and an admittance of vulnerability. But these are the lies of the enemy.

You *must* forgive. It is a witness of Christ's strength and courage inside of you.

If appropriate, go to your wife and your children and ask them to forgive you for your offenses against them. Like the other things you take seriously, do this well too! Not half-hearted or an apology along with a caveat that shares the blame.

This demonstrates your growth and shows you are *Man Enough to Forgive*, to ask for forgiveness, and without shame to pivot and fix your own shortcomings.

This is incredibly important to model with your family, particularly for your children. Work on reconciliation and healing in those relationships. Your family needs to see and experience forgiveness in your life so they too learn to forgive. Show them how it's done!

It is a sign of strength, not weakness.

BREAKING THE CYCLE OF FAMILY BROKENNESS

When we refuse to keep the family structure intact as God designed, we create a deep brokenness that not only affects us but our entire family both now and for generations to come. Remember, the thoughts of the kids are "better off", does not mean "well" given God is not a liar.

Cycle Breaker

You have the ability and responsibility to help break this destructive cycle - the cycle *you* likely have also experienced the negative multi-generational effects. If you repeat the abandonment or refuse to be the man God created you to be, then your children will suffer the wounds of abandonment too.

The brokenness of divorce is not a legacy that honors God Almighty.

This cycle can be broken when you refuse to repeat the mistakes and sins of others. Now is the time! Don't look back.

It is possible that even as you read this you can see how you have already continued this cycle in your own family or *you* broke your family and it needs repair. It is never too late to begin to restore and heal what has been broken. This whole book has been walking you through the steps needed to forgive your earthly father. Do that first and then tackle the repair of family relationships next, with great energy, hope, and yes, intentionality.

Your Heavenly Father and the Holy Spirit is with you.

Get Real

Take this time of learning and reflection to anticipate your family's perspective and their assessment of the relationship with you. Would they say, "I need to forgive my father, husband, etc.?"

If so, considering their point of view, go to them now and ask them to forgive you. Realize they might not yet have processed these hurts and deficiencies with the understanding *you've* developed by going through the learning, growing, and healing stages covered in *Man Enough to Forgive*. They may not be in a heart and head space to forgive you right away, but you need to take that first step.

It's up to <u>you</u> to break the vicious cycle. Without shame, repair and heal what has been broken to the extent it is in your power. Pray and ask the Holy Spirit to work in your life and those in this cycle with you. Forgiveness takes the help of the Holy Spirit and the proactive intentionality of your efforts. It's that plain and simple.

Man to Man

I feel compelled to camp here just for a minute. Brothers, this is the whole point of *Man Enough to Forgive*, so it is critically important to me that you "get it."

I wrote this book… I *had* to write this book because I am *just like you*.

I'll bet we share more life storylines than you'd imagine – especially with the process of becoming the men God wants us to be and the things in family life that matter most. I was hurt deeply as a child and carried that into adulthood because I didn't know how to understand how to process it or how to intentionally address it. I made some choices that for years got in the way of my relationship with my wife, children, and it hurt others as well.

Worldly success and having a family of my own didn't stop me from rolling down a path that could have perpetuated the generational brokenness I experienced – becoming just another broken man with a broken family – another statistic.

I felt like a man, but I wasn't *Man Enough to Forgive* until the Lord got ahold of me and the Holy Spirit showed me true forgiveness of the Heavenly Father through the forgiveness of my earthly father.

As you've learned in this book, to get to the forgiveness part, we have to go through all the steps and stages, some very painful, that precede the actual forgiveness. This necessary exposure to the bare truth is vital to understand and confront reality.

And I'll be honest, at the time I'd have preferred to do just about anything <u>but</u> forgive my father. But in doing so, God unleashed an entirely new, brightly lit path for my life – a different and *better* destiny for myself and my family. With that transformation came the call to share this simple but not-so-easy path to freedom that eludes at least half the men in America (and probably many more!).

My heart aches for these men who are in bondage, but it breaks even more for the families that'll pay the price for his pain and are destined to repeat the sins of the father. Please join me on the other side of your pain. You can do this! I believe in you.

I'll say it again - break the cycle. Forgive your earthly father for abandoning you, for not being the man God created him to be and seek the forgiveness of those you have wronged through your selfish sinful actions. Imitate God!

Focus on your Heavenly Father

Your relationship with your earthly father might be beyond repair.

The vast majority of fatherless boys have a secret fantasy where their dad returns to them, apologizes for being terrible, vows to fix everything and then goes on to be the world's greatest dad. It is time to bury that dream. Not because it is impossible, though it might very well be, but because it is not real and it takes your focus away from where it needs to be. Plus, that fantasy is still reactive, contingent on the actions of someone else. That hope may have been more appropriate when you were a boy and dependent on your father, but you're a *man* now. It's your time to take control. Wait no longer and to get the healing going and into the next gear.

Your Heavenly Father will NEVER LEAVE or FORSAKE you. He loves you and has begun the change in you to make you more like the Jesus. He's set you about the task of taking the message of salvation to the world. By forgiving your earthly father and focusing on your Heavenly Father's Kingdom you not only experience healing but become an agent of healing.

The old you, the one who was selfish, the victim, and self-centered is gone; the new man you are in Christ is here and you need to live in that spectacular truth. Not in your past or your earthly understanding or feelings. What a blessing it is to break the old cycle and start down the path that leads you to the Kingdom of Heaven. In this Kingdom, you are called a son of the living God (Romans 8:14-16). To us he is "Abba" or "Daddy," the Father who leads us to becoming the men He created us to be.

There are only Victors in God's Kingdom.

| Chapter 11: Study |

NEXT STEPS: Working through the chapter

a. How can I better provide for my family?

b. How can I better Pastor my family? What day will I set for family bible study? Etc.

c. How can I better protect my family?

d. Does my church have tools?

e. I can model forgiveness in my life by (*ways*).

f. The cycle of family brokenness for me is (*symptoms*). I can work on breaking the cycle by doing (*actions*).

GET ROLLING with the Companion Guide: Preparation to write a *Forgiveness Letter*:

- Utilize the *Man Enough to Forgive* Personal Study Journal workbook

| Scripture References |

1. Men need women to be complete in their calling the same way that women needed men to pastor, provide and protect her.
Genesis 2:20-25; 4:1 (NASB)

2. God intends for the man and woman to become one person in body, mind and spirit. Genesis 2:24; Matthew 19:5 (NASB)

3. Man and wife are designed to be together for life. Proverbs 14:26-27 (NASB)

4. Husbands must love and honor their wives. 1 Peter 3:7-8 (ESV)

5. Children are to honor and obey their parents. Ephesians 6:1-4 (NASB)

6. Apostle Paul recounts the qualities of a godly man. 1 Timothy 3:2-4 (ESV)

7. Wives must be devoted to their husbands and children in the same way they are devotes to Christ. Ephesians 5:22-23 (NASB)

8. Wives should submit to husbands as the Church to Christ. Ephesians 5:22-24 (ESV)

9. Apostle Paul compares family life to the Church. Ephesians 5:17-33 (NASB)

10. Christ is the head of man, man of his wife, and Christ's head is God. 1 Corinthians (NASB)

11. Men need to teach their family to pray each day. 1 Timothy 5:17 (NASB)

12. We must imitate Christ in our life and put others' needs before our own. 1 Corinthians 11:1 (NASB)

13. As men, we should be servant leaders, treating others in need like we would Christ. Matthew 25:31-46 (NASB)

14. Christ even appealed with the Heavenly Father for forgiveness of those who crucified Him. Luke 23:34 (NASB)

15. When you break the pattern of sin and unforgiveness, you are called a son of the living God. Romans 8:14-16 (NASB)

heroic

[he·ro·ic] **adjective**

God must be the Hero. Our uncompromising faith, fortitude, courage, perseverance, and sacrifice are limited without our reliance on God. In our weakness, God is glorified. God promises to be our Hero in our fear.

CHAPTER TWELVE

Your Forgiveness Letter

"How blessed is he whose transgression is forgiven,
Whose sin is covered!
How blessed is the man to whom the Lord does not impute iniquity,
And in whose spirit there is no deceit!
When I kept silent about my sin, my body wasted away
Through my groaning all day long."
1 Corinthians 11:1-3 (NASB)

| The Finish Line |

Stop making excuses for not charging the hill in courageous strength through Christ.

We often take the easy path in life, avoiding conflict and hardship whenever possible. Some men are better at cruising and ducking out than others, but to some extent we are all guilty of avoiding pain – even when it is necessary. Heck, for some people, seeking comfort is the *whole* game of life. This is part of our fleshly nature we combat as we are presented hard truths of God. Remember, being the victim becomes an identity as defense barrier.

As we mature and grow both physically and spiritually from boys into men, to become the man the Lord created you to be, we must be willing to embrace challenges and do the hard work when it's the *right* thing and the *Christ-like* thing to do. Your feelings, your habits your emotional scars need to stop being an excuse.

My goal in your journey thus far with *Man Enough to Forgive* has been to guide you in asking the tough questions behind your wounded heart so that you can face the truth in ways you might have been avoiding for years. This chapter is no different. In many ways, this is the finishing leg of the marathon - the final push that despite being so close to the finishing line some runners get fatigued and quit.

Be courageous, be God's man. Not our will, but God's will is our master.

What an incredible shame it is when men who have come this far but choose not to go all the way. I'm running alongside you.

Your goal is ahead. Dig deep and finish strong!

THE HOLY SPIRIT

As sinful people, how do we learn to imitate God in this way?

In my view, without God's intervention it is impossible to fully forgive your earthly father after all the wrong and hurt his sin has caused you. We cannot merely "suck it up" or "man up" and move forward. We must be sure to truly and completely forgive so that God will be honored by our actions and receive the glory that only He deserves.

Unforgiveness is a deep, destructive sin. God will not be mocked. Sin breaks our fellowship with a Holy God, even our ABBA Father.

A Greater Power

For this challenge we have been blessed with the Holy Spirit. Thank you, Lord for this blessing and power through you.

God Himself dwells in each of us, giving us the divine power needed to perform such a momentous task. According to the Scripture, it is the Holy

Spirit who helps Christians to understand both the Love of God in Christ and the depth of His forgiveness of our sins (Ephesians 1). This understanding leads us to strive to be more like God in how we live. The Holy Spirit helps us to be faithful and obey the command to forgive, just as we want to be forgiven (Matthew 6:14-15).

Without the Holy Spirit convicting our hearts and drawing us towards Christ we will never be able to forgive to the standard of God's Word (John 16:7-11). True biblical forgiveness is a direct work of the Holy Spirit in the life of the Believer.

Therefore, begin to pray specifically for this strength to acknowledge and to forgive this deep sin.

Summon Your Helper

Prayer is powerful. It is a vital ministry we must uphold.

In fact, it is one of the least used but most powerful tool in our life's workshop. It's a blessing with no cost, no barrier between you and your Creator, and no limits to how often it can be utilized to connect you with Him. The enemy hopes you do _not_ pray.

Trust me, with the Devil's desire to isolate you and to cut you off from your source of love, support, and wisdom, he'll tell you that you don't need to forgive and you can 'do life' on your own. Nonsense! Be on your knees praying and asking for guidance and wisdom as you compose each part of the letter.

If you sense you cannot pray _specifically_ in this regard, this should highlight to you that you do not want to let this hurt and identity go.

Here are a few suggestions as you write:

1. **Take your time**. This is incredibly important. No matter how anxious you are to be done and over the whole ordeal, give the process sufficient space to really reflect all you need to share.

2. **Pray.** As mentioned before, pray before, during, and after writing the letter. Not only will you receive the guidance in your spirit that you seek, but you won't feel alone while doing it.

3. **Be "all in."** You've come this far. Your letter will mean more to both you and your father if it clearly includes your reflection and transparently opens up about the damage that was done to you by your father's choice to abandon/hurt you, and also about your relationship with the Lord and your motivation to forgive.

4. **Get feedback.** When it is finished, share your letter with those closest to you. Ensure that it makes sense to someone outside of yourself. Make any edits as necessary.

5. **Copy, archive, and send.** Make a copy for yourself and then send the original to your father, if possible. If your father has died or you can't make contact with him, mail it to your pastor, a close friend, someone who will understand the depth of what you have written. There is tremendous freedom in finally dropping that letter in the mailbox. At that point you can say, "I have forgiven my father. As this letter goes into the mail I am free of the burden of unforgiveness towards him."

6. **Now, start praying.** Pray for your father and his eternal salvation.

Additional Suggestions:

- **Celebrate your newfound freedom.** Rejoice over this powerful moment in your life. Reframe what it means to be forgiven and to forgive. You've moved from anger to compassion, from bitterness to love, from less-than to more-than, and from hurt to healing!

Such a righteous masculinity, restored in fellowship to the Heavenly Father, that revives the soul.

Through your forgiveness, you're gaining and demonstrating so much:

- It's a testament to your maturity.

- It is a reflection of your faith walk and relationship with the Lord.

- It unlocks your own ability to be forgiven.

- It breaks the chains of your pain.

- It frees you of the excuses you have blamed past behavior on.

- It sets a positive example for others in your life (and for your father).

• **Share your forgiveness with your children.** If you have children, they may not have been aware of the pain and struggle you've borne throughout your life as a result of the abandonment of your father. Now is a good time to share the whole story with them and to teach them what it looks like to be *Man Enough to Forgive*.

• **Keep your Forgiveness Letter close.** It may be helpful to occasionally refer to your letter, especially if past resentment or triggers knock at your heart's door. Remind yourself of what you've forgiven, why you've forgiven, and how you are committed to never revert or to compromise that forgiveness. You've invested too much to give up God's truths of who you are, in Him!

• **Welcome help from your support system.** Between the ever-present friend you have in the Holy Spirit and your own network of supporters, whether that be your spouse, a mentor, men's group, or a pastor, don't hesitate to ask for help. Men need accountability, both to submit to the Lord's command and to live up to our own goals and commitments over time.

COMPONENTS OF YOUR *FORGIVENESS LETTER*

Getting it done!

This section helps you to compile all the components from the study sections of the previous chapters. In the end, it is *your* letter so think of this as a rough outline suggestion. Pray for guidance from the Holy Spirit and be honest with yourself.

Series Four | Chapter Twelve | Your Forgiveness Letter

Write your *Forgiveness Letter*.

Again, I encourage you to utilize the companion <u>Personal Study Journal</u> to help flush out your approach to your Forgiveness Letter and to follow an easy to follow structure.

Take your time and pray along the way. Here are some considerations to think about:

- How will you address your father in the letter? i.e. As Dad, by his first name, dear Jerk, dear Abandoner, etc.?

- What will your opening sentence be?

- Tell you father about your emotional trials, your hurts, anger, and sadness. Be honest about how his actions directly affected you and others in your life.

- Address the broken promises he made to you and how this impacted you.

- Will you ask questions of him? If so, craft questions that cannot be answered by a "yes" or "no" response, but instead would require some dialog and explanation.

- Share the biblical model of forgiveness and how it has changed your life and brought personal healing.

- Share the Gospel message, hope for salvation, and your earnest prayers for him with your father.

- Close your letter. Put the ball in his court to take the next step.

* Rest. You have done your part in honoring your Savior, your Lord, and your Heavenly Father.

My *Forgiveness Letter*

You should know that for me to come to a forgiving place and to write my father's forgiveness letter was one of the most peaceful and yet, most important things I've done in my adult life.

I too had the ego and self-righteousness issues to overcome. The devil wanted me to stop by whispering once again in my ear, "your father left you, he hurt you, why forgive him?"

It took all the help from the Holy Spirit that I've mentioned to get me over myself and my entitlement to resentment over forgiveness. I had to get to a place of submission and obedience by the work of Holy Spirit.

Now, I praise in thankfulness to the Lord for this very special day. He faithfully led me and carried me through this necessary threshold to genuine, complete, and demonstrated forgiveness. He'll do the same for you.

Please read my Forgiveness Letter at the end of this book.

I hope it serves as an example and helps you as you formulate your own letter. I am praying that God has brought you to a place where you can write the letter. I completely know and recognize this is an act of the Holy Spirit. I am pulling for you!

KNOWING WHEN YOU HAVE TRULY FORGIVEN

This is key. A step of genuine self-reflection. Most do not want to self-assess this command by God. They avoid, because they know, they cannot lie to God.

However, we tell ourselves and others, "Yes, I forgave them" in our quickness to appear true to our faith. Don't be that guy. <u>Know</u> that you have with every soul fiber in your body.

During my presentations on this subject, the most frequent question I get is how do I know I have truly forgiven my father.

This is what I ask them.

1. Have you written your forgiveness down in a letter and given to your father? If he is dead, have you given the letter to your mom, your sister, your brother, your mentor, your pastor?

2. Are you faithfully praying for his salvation?

If not, it is my deeply held opinion, that they have not. There is something very profound when you put your forgiveness in writing, share it, and make it known.

One of the basic reasons is now others can read the words you used, and how you presented your forgiveness. Your faithful forgiveness words are straightforward and is very easy to understand if it is genuine.

Did you honor God in forgiveness by not conditionally forgiving?

Did you soft-sell, gloss over hard truths?

Was it done in biblical love?

We are called to be soulfully authentic in our confessions and testimony in Christ. We are called to earnestly pray for our enemies.

Publicly sharing with others – like I have done in this book - that you have forgiven is a good step that adds some accountability to this decision, but it also needs to be lived out in action.

The Fellowship of Christian Brotherhood

There's another important element of forgiving your father that many men overlook. Your hurt, pain, and resentment has driven a deep wedge between you and your father. Heck, it might even be a Grand Canyon.

But forgiveness levels the field between the two of you. It is a recognition that you are both sinners. We are equal in our shortcomings before the

Lord – if not equal in the actual sins that were committed. Forgiving frees both parties to be forgiven.

Secondly, based on your forgiveness, (regardless if your father is cooperating with reconciliation,) by removing the barrier of unforgiveness that may set him outside your ecosystem of people with whom you normally share fellowship. You should want for your father, as you would with any friend, family member, your children, co-workers etc. to be in an active faith relationship with the Heavenly Father.

As mentioned in earlier chapter, there should be discerning caution, or even a strict barrier when the offender, even if your father, when gross evil was perpetrated or if evil, illicit, destructive sin is ongoing. Remember, biblical forgiveness is different than earthly reconciliation.

You'll *want* to pray for him. You'll pray for his well-being, for his spiritual development, and for his soul. And with pure intent you'll desperately want to see your father saved, a member of the fellowship of Christian brotherhood.

Yes, you'll want all these things for the man who hurt you so deeply. The guy who you hated.

You'll want to see him as we walk the streets of Heaven and fall to our knees together, equal before the Lord. Just as Jesus' compassion and desire for restoration was extended to thieves who hung on crosses next to him and to the Romans and Jews who crucified him, you will want your dad to be made clean and pure through the Father's forgiveness and to join you in paradise.

There are as many scenarios and unique conditions of your relationship with your father as there are men reading this book.

The truth is we often *say* that we have forgiven someone but then still bring up past offenses when our scars are bumped, when we're situationally triggered, or when that person wrongs us again. Instead, we need to be disciplined and hold ourselves to a forgiveness standard that is modeled by God.

In Psalm 103:10-12 we are told that when God forgives our sins they are "as far as the east is from the west." He never brings them back up once they are forgiven.

As imitators of God we must act similarly when we forgive.

Here is another way to know if you have truly forgiven your father. If you stood face-to-face with him today, would you share the Gospel with him? Do you want him to come to faith in Christ and spend eternity with the Lord and with you? Would you welcome him into the fellowship of Christian brotherhood?

If you answer "no" to any of those questions - you haven't forgiven him.

Truly forgiving means that you *reject* the sinful desire for vengeance and *suppress* the feeling of self-righteousness that places you as better than him. True forgiveness will be demonstrated by an enduring desire for your father's redeemed soul, wanting the best for him - even if it is at your emotional comfort. After you have forgiven him, your dad's abandonment of you/sinful actions are in the past. As such, you need to stop focusing on this and move forward towards God even if you have an emotional limp from the past.

I bump my abandonment scars now and then, it may make me tear up some, but now it just reminds me of how much forgiveness I have received and that a Holy God would save and forgive a wretch like me.

I rest in the arms and grace of my Heavenly Father now, with the comfort and peace knowing He has adopted me, will Never Leave or Forsake me, and has a mansion in Heaven where He is preparing a room for me.

Do not let anything, even unforgiveness, stand in the way of hearing the words from your ABBA Father, "Well done, good and faithful servant".

IT IS FINISHED

> *"He said, 'It is finished!' And He bowed His head and gave up His spirit."* John 19:30 (NASB)

Conclusion

Over the course of this book I have tried to help you see a great many truths, even hard, counter-cultural truths.

My mission, with the goal that you will come to a place through Christ, where you can truly forgive your earthly father. The pain of abandonment and the wounds you suffered will still surface occasionally even after they heal. But trust me, it will be less and less and your joy, the peace that surpasses all understanding will grow.

My heart beats for the fatherless boys in their distress across our nation. God redeemed me to be a vocal, bold Advocate for those left behind to fend for themselves. Those who are crying themselves to sleep in their pain, loneliness and anger. Those pleading for help to be shepherded into manhood because they know in their soul, they are on a destructive path.

Once you are healed, please courageously jump back into the Kingdom battle, get back on the field doing work that lasts an eternity. Satan wants to keep you on the sidelines, in the hospital of wounded souls, and out of this special brotherhood of righteous warriors swinging the sword of grace and truth.

You were born with a glorious purpose, you are not a mistake. Be proud to put on the full armor of God Almighty and be the man God intended for you to be. Charge up the hill into the fight.

Know that, your brothers and me are waiting for re-enforcements as we are behind enemy lines. We are battling daily to reach and recuse those boys, those men - our Great Adversary - has wounded deeply and holding captive. We need your masculine, bold, and self-sacrificing help.

I am thankful God made men willing to die on the hill of righteousness. Those who do not care what this corrupt, broken and perverse culture has to say about them. We take our orders from our Creator by faithfully following the One True King, the King of Kings, the Lord of Lords.

Charge!

Chapter 12: Study

NEXT STEPS: Working through the chapter

a. What's left to contemplate?

b. It is time to act and follow Christ's example.

c. It is decision time. How will your heart respond? Hard as stone, or soft as flesh?

GET ROLLING with the <u>Companion Guide</u>: Preparation to write a *Forgiveness Letter*:

- Utilize the *Man Enough to Forgive* Personal Study Journal workbook

Scripture References

1. The Holy Spirit helps us understand Christ's love and the depth of his forgiveness of our sins. Ephesians 1 (NASB)

2. The Holy Spirit helps us to be faithful and obey the command to forgive. Matthew 6:14-15 (NASB)

3. Without the Holy Spirit convicting our hearts and drawing us towards Christ we will never be able to forgive to the standard of God's Word. John 16:7-11 (NASB)

4. When God forgives our sins, he does so permanently. Psalm 103:10-12 (NASB)

5. On earth, Jesus got the job done. He ran the whole race. He didn't give up. He gave and forgave all. John 19:30 (NASB)

6. When we feel weak, the Word of God tells us to lean on the Holy Spirit for strength and support. 1 Corinthians 12 (ESV).

APPENDIX

My Forgiveness Letter Example

| A fatherless boy |

March 2003

Dear Dad,

I write this letter in sincere trepidation, but relieved sorrow. I have been living with the deepest pain, anger and disappointment over your abandonment of Kym and me–I was just born and Kym was three years old. I will be forty this October.

I write this letter to wash clean my wound that I did not know how to heal until now. I want you to know that I entered this life and grew up without a father to hold me, protect me, guide me into manhood or to sacrifice for me. Instead, you gave your son up for some other convenient life. Your love and time went to others for which you gave up as well. Therefore, so you understand completely, you abandoned Kym and me for something you threw away. Again, you abandoned Kym and me for something you threw away. Those are powerful actions with a profound meaning to living souls. Deep wounds that you created that I am now able to heal. However, I now realize I will never have that opportunity with you, time has gone by. This is painful to write, but so necessary.

As I unburden and heal my soul, I do want you to know where I am coming from and the purpose of this letter. I want you to know, that what you did was terribly wrong, it mattered greatly in my life, and that I have come to forgive you.

As I hold my son and daughters, I could not even imagine turning them over to the world without me there. I did not understand fully why this deep wound and hurt would not heal. My anger has grown inside me as I see me in my son. The scabs have finally been torn off for the last time. As I catch my children in my arms as I arrive home from work, as I read to my children, comfort them during periods of pain, experience their daily achievements, participate in their memories, and to honestly, completely be there for them as a father is called to do, I understand where my anger and hurt is coming from. I have said I love you all my life as something I was supposed to do, out of respect. It was not a love I now know should have existed. I bristle every time you say I acted a certain way as a baby when you referring to my John Spencer. You were not there. You would not know. I do not have childhood memories, stories or traditions to share about my father with my children. But rather, I have confusion and questions I cannot answer to myself or family. Not once have you ever explained, shown remorse, regret, or discussed your actions. Kym and I have done all of the sacrificing for you and on your behalf.

I thank the Lord and Savior for the angels he sent to watch over me. They have always been there and I give thanks every night. I thank my mom for being such a strong person and caring mother. My love for her could not be any stronger. She gave unconditionally and sacrificed totally of herself for her children. I saw her joy and love for us through all her unselfish pain and loneliness as she made decisions out of necessity. I saw my big sister starve for love for a father that was not there for her. Her search took painful directions. I am so proud of her for being so strong and becoming such a loving person.

I love my memories of my Uncle Bucky. He was the man of my life growing up. I learned from him as I grew up in search of what it meant to be a man. I learned to be fun from him. He took the time to be our Santa Claus. I felt the joy of throwing a baseball as high as I could to him and felt the thrill of catching the baseball that touched the stars from him. He gave me confidence and I will forever be grateful to him. Where were you? Devoting all your time and energy to others and not your children-only to lose it all. I do not understand.

Your efforts toward me as I was older have been noticed, but I have been unable to fully accept or appreciate them. I now know why. There is no foundation to build on. I would, however, like to share with you a moment I cherish deeply. A son needs to know his name-who he is in this world. Upon me entering high school, you made it clear to me you wanted me to use my birth name-Smithbaker. You gave me the courage to fight for that name and I got it changed my freshman year. I remember saying to myself, I now, at least know my name - I know who I am. As symbolic as it may sound, it meant everything to me at that time. And, it still does.

I cry as I write this, tears of yesterday's pain and tears of wounds healed. I have a selfish prayer... I pray for your soul that you may find our Lord, Jesus so that we will not be separated again upon departure from this earth. Father and son are meant to be together. It is a gift from God that should not be thrown away.

Thank you for reading this and I truly hope you understand my purpose. It is my prayer that in the time remaining, we can have a relationship that deepens.

Your son, John Joseph Smithbaker, III

Appendix | My Forgiveness Letter Example

"You are nothing better than deceitful hypocrites if you harbor in your minds a single unforgiving thought. There are some sins which may be in your heart, and yet you may be saved. But you cannot be saved unless you are forgiving. If we do not choose to forgive, we choose to be damned."

Pastor Charles Spurgeon

The Companion 4-part Series Personal or Group Study Guide

A MASCULINE CHALLENGE

Being a MAN, born MALE, and the unique traits of MASCULINITY all have special places and divine roles in the Heavenly Father's creation. It is time that we recapture God's holy definitions from the lies of this world.

We've had enough haven't we, Men? Enough of the soft, passive, and safe men's group studies where guys sit around and chat about stuff but never activate or accomplish anything great for the Kingdom by following the King of Kings' directives. And guess what? The church body of believers is sick and tired of men just talking.

Let's be MEN OF ACTION. Let's TAKE BACK TERRITORY for the Lord's Kingdom. Let's be willing to GO BEHIND ENEMY LINES to rescue the lost.

My brave brothers in the Lord, there'll be no beating around the bush here. No fluff. No excuses. No vagueness.

No fear of truth. This journey is for courageous Men of God and Men of Action. It'll flush out the posers, flakes, and fakes.

This study will challenge you. "Bring it on!" you say. Great! Here we go.

The first challenge is: Making a COMMITMENT to this study journey.

❯ For more information go to: www.manenoughtoforgive.com

Another book by John J. Smithbaker
The Great American Rescue Mission™

Fatherlessness is the #1 societal issue that is decimating the family and tearing at the very fabric of America.

In his new book, **The Great American Rescue Mission**, ministry founder John Smithbaker shares how *Fathers in the Field* engages the local church to reach, rescue, and restore fatherless boys in their community to end the epidemic of generational fatherlessness.

For more information go to: www.fathersinthefield.com/the-great-american-rescue-mission/

ABOUT THE AUTHOR

John Smithbaker

| A fatherless boy |

Even before he was born, the conditions for John Smithbaker's ministry training began. While still in his mother's womb, John's biological father abandoned their family and left them to fend for themselves. As a young boy, teen, and well into his adult life, the dark hole that bored through John's heart grew. Try as he did to camouflage the deepest of soul wounds through an unrelenting pursuit of personal success and worldly accomplishments; nothing could fill the void left by not having God's fatherhood plan in his life.

One fateful night on route to a fishing expedition, John's life was changed forever. In his "Damascus Road" moment, the Heavenly Father clarified to John the nature of his pain, the profound magnitude of the fatherless epidemic among boys and men, and what needed to be done next. However, like so many who are terribly hurt, John largely externalized his pain and held fast to a fatherless upbringing and his broken home. Then, John's worst of sins flashed before him in repentance on the side of the road. Finally, at the prompting of the Holy Spirit, he gave up his commitment to pain and resentment and repented for the deepest sin in a fatherless boy's life – the unforgiveness of his father.

Soon after his saving-faith conversion, John was called by the Lord to abandon his worldly pursuits of a successful CEO in business to become a full-time missionary. God commissioned John to become a national advocate for the precious fatherless who have no voice. As a result, John developed and launched the life-impacting *Fathers in the Field* ministry to bring God's redemptive love to boys and men across America through the local church.

A gifted leader combines his personal experience and straight-forward style to connect and speak with men held back from becoming the man God designed who suffers through the brokenness, the pain, and the anger of being left behind.

As an author, speaker, *Fathers in the Field's* founding servant, and an Alpha male activator, John's passion, and focus are to help men recapture their divinely assigned roles of Pastor, Provider, and Protector in the home, as well as in the church. Standing in the gap for the fatherless and challenging men to defend those under their care is a call on his life from the Heavenly Father.

...

Rob Goff

Rob has served the Lord in ministry for over 30 years as a Pastor, missionary, and professor. He has decades of experience in the mission fields of the fatherless – both in foreign lands and in our nation. Rob has dedicated himself to discipling fatherless boys and men and working with them to do the same.

Rob holds both an MDiv and a Master of Theology degree. He currently oversees extended Christian Education for Grace Matters, a counseling ministry. He has a passion for seeing Christians come to a deep understanding of their faith and experience the life changes that come with faithfulness to Christ Jesus, knowing that this devotion will manifest itself in serving the fatherless and the widow.